HOW TO WRITE
ADVERTISING FEATURES

HOW TO WRITE ADVERTISING FEATURES

John Paxton Sheriff

a&b

First published in Great Britain in 1995 by
Allison & Busby
an imprint of Wilson & Day Ltd
179 King's Cross Road
London WC1X 9BZ

A catalogue record for this book is available from
the British Library.

ISBN 0 74900 210 7

Designed and typeset by N-J Design Associates
Romsey, Hampshire
Printed and bound in Great Britain by
Redwood Books, Trowbridge, Wiltshire

CONTENTS

1

THE ADVERTISING FEATURE

Most aspiring writers will have come across two anecdotes that tend to infuriate the beginner.

The first is attributed to American Nobel Prize winner, Sinclair Lewis. When faced with a class of eager students, he asked them if they sincerely wanted to learn to write. On receiving the expected answer, his retort was devastating. 'O.K.' said Mr Lewis. 'So why aren't you all at home writing?' (Incidentally, that's a weak, watered-down version; he's reputed to have been drunk at the time!)

The second is from Boswell's *Life of Samuel Johnson*, in which the great man is quoted as saying that, 'No man but a blockhead ever wrote except for money'.

Those two quotations hoist the average beginners' blood pressure a few notches because they know that sitting at home writing can be tough when everything you send out comes back with a rejection slip. Achieving Samuel Johnson's ideal state by doing what Sinclair Lewis suggests always seems to be something that happens to other writers.

What I have tried to achieve in this book is to get the novice writer, the frustrated writer, or the writer unsure of which direction to take, over both those hurdles. I want you to sit at home writing. And I want you to get paid for what you write.

By approaching your writing from a different angle – one that you may never have considered before – it's possible to sit with pen and paper, typewriter or word processor, and thoroughly enjoy your writing because you know that everything you write will sell. The reason everything will sell is because each piece of writing you work on will have been commissioned by an editor – and that means there'll be a welcome cheque popping through the

1

letter box at the end of every month. Another frequently heard complaint is that writing is a solitary occupation. We'll lay that ghost, too.

By diligently studying the chapters in this book, and by careful application of the principles laid down, you'll regularly see your writing in print and you'll meet a lot of new people every week. The way you'll scale that personal Everest is by becoming a freelance correspondent, writing short advertising features for your local newspapers.

'Hmmm,' I hear you say. 'And what exactly is a short advertising feature?'

I'll be the first to admit that it needs a style of writing that may be a long way removed from that required for short stories, novels, or general articles. But it will get you into print, it will bring you a regular income (though it won't make you rich), and it has other important benefits which we will come to a little later.

One important advantage that makes this kind of work particularly attractive is the extreme flexibility of the working hours. Within limits you will be able to fit the writing/interviewing time into your own busy schedule – and that makes it ideal for people with young children, single parents, people already working at one part-time job, and many others for whom regular full-time employment is out of the question.

Depending on your expectations it can also, as we shall see later, provide a most reasonable full-time income while retaining that attractive flexibility.

In this first chapter I'll introduce you to advertising feature writing, show how businesses and newspapers work together, dwell briefly on the writer's role, and point to several key elements that make it an ideal way to begin professional writing.

The subjects covered will include:

- What is an advertising feature?
- Will writing them improve writing skills?
- What income can be expected.
- Who needs advertising features?
- Which publications run regular advertising features?
- What newspaper staff are involved?
- Who writes the features?

What is an Advertising Feature?

Format

If you glance through most regional daily or weekly newspapers you will come across one or more full or half-pages dedicated to advertising features. The format is pretty standard.

Each will be clearly labelled as an ADVERTISING FEATURE. There will be a central section devoted to TEXT, one or more PHOTOGRAPHS, and a number of BOX (DISPLAY) ADVERTISEMENTS filling up the remaining space. The text and photographs will relate to the main business being advertised. The firms or individuals taking out a box advertisement will mention that they supply, support, or are in some way connected with the business being featured.

For example, a recent half-page featured a new business retailing motor spares. Among the supporting box advertisements were other similar dealers (wishing him luck), a car hi-fi dealer (a supplier), a car-body repairer and a petroleum company (both related businesses).

Content

The amount of text will depend on a number of factors.

Most newspapers of the kind we are considering will be tabloids, and a full-page advertising feature will rarely have more than 500 words of text. Quite often there will be fewer, and the space will be filled with extra photographs or more support ads.

A half-page advertising feature will use about 350 words of text. If the newspaper is a broadsheet, then those figures will be increased, though not necessarily doubled.

Sometimes a business will take out two or even four pages, perhaps to advertise a major expansion, a change of status to a limited company, or a move to new premises. In such cases the text may be divided into sections, typical examples of which might cover company history; current trading position; how expansion will improve the company; and plans for the future.

3

Business to business

Where the advertising feature differs from a normal full or half-page advertisement is that the space is paid for by the supporting box advertisements. The business to be featured is approached by the newspaper's advertising representatives and, when the format has been agreed, the business gives the newspaper a list of its suppliers. These are then 'chased' by the representatives.

This may seem to place an unfair burden on the supporting firms. So what often happens is that similar businesses are grouped on the same page and over a six- or eight-week cycle, each has its turn to hold centre stage. In many cases this regular page will be given a title. DINING OUT would feature hotels and restaurants. SPARES AND REPAIRS would deal with garages and car dealers. SPORT FOR ALL would do the rounds of leisure centres and sports clubs.

You, the writer

From the above it will be clear that writing advertising features can be of absorbing interest, with a new challenge to be met with each assignment. Commissions to write features about a newly opened fast-food outlet will be interspersed with others which take you out and about. Some will frequently involve meetings with managing directors of multi-national firms or the chief executives of county councils.

You can make valuable personal contacts which can be of great use in your everyday life and help with other writing interests. Because each business – even within a common group – can be vastly different from its nearest competitor, writing styles need to be chosen with care, and adapted to suit exactly the needs of each client.

Will writing them improve writing skill?

Everybody will have their own answer to that one.

4

The dedicated fiction writer will be convinced that no possible good can come from writing 500 words about, say, a high-street launderette. The magazine article writer accustomed to crafting 1500-word masterpieces will say that in 500 words you scarcely have time to get past the opening – and, besides, the pay is rubbish. And the staff writer on a busy newspaper – while saying little because he's a professional and knows he can be roped in to do your job if you're ever indisposed – probably classes you as some sort of hack who isn't quite good enough to be a 'proper' journalist.

The truth, as I have learnt from experience, is that regularly writing advertising features provides first-class training in the writing skills and disciplines essential for anyone hoping to develop into a full-time, professional writer. Even if your sights are set a little lower than that, perhaps the ambition to have the occasional short story published by one of the women's glossies, those same qualities are required if you are to have any hope of success.

Excellent training

There is only one sure way to become a writer – and that's by writing.

As a freelance correspondent writing advertising features, you already have the incentive. You know you're going to get paid. You will to a certain extent set your own work schedules. But you will be working to deadlines. Each time you sit at your typewriter you will have set a time – one hour, two hours, four hours, or much longer – within which the work must be finished. You must produce 500 words of publishable text. Finished copy. Ready to be typeset. Or very nearly.

You develop the facility for writing quickly and accurately, revising as you go, then polishing the final draft.

As well as having time limits, you will be writing to a specified word count. Within those additional limits you must present a lot of facts in a logical yet interesting way. This will teach you to select your words with care. You will need to choose words that will convey your meaning – exactly – but at the same time you must be descriptive, always painting a convincing word picture that manages to extol the virtues of the business you are advertising. Please note that word 'extol'. You will be writing for a newspaper readership, and all such words are ruled out. You must select only those words that will be easily understood by all your readers. Never use a long word when a short one will do the job, or an obscure one when there is a familiar alternative.

As a professional writer, writer's block will be something that used to happen to you but which now you cannot afford. True, you will have your own notes to work from (most of the time), which makes life easier. But there is still the need to bring freshness and originality to the opening of each short feature, to work through it with imagination and to close in a way that will leave the readers satisfied.

A word of caution, here. I say there is a need to bring freshness to your work, but the truth is that you can probably get away with writing well below your best. Many published advertising features are badly written. It's a job like any other. Repetition can create boredom. Each feature can become a task to complete in the shortest possible time and, perhaps faced with writers who are content to take the money and run, busy editors uneasily make do with what they get.

Please don't fall into that trap. Throughout this book I want you to look on this form of writing as a means to an end. Several ends, perhaps: money, your own byline (your name as writer), and some local recognition. But the main aim must always be to improve all areas of your writing, and eventually to move on to success in other fields. And that means producing your best work, every time.

There will often be the temptation to write only as well as is necessary. But believe me, when your work appears in print you'll see glaring faults in even your finest writing, and that always delivers the sharp kick that makes you vow to do better.

The genuine article

I said, tongue in cheek, that an advertising feature is unlike a short story or 'proper' article. But each of those features will have a structure that is remarkably similar to its bigger brothers (I'm thinking of articles now, rather than stories), and in Chapter 6 I will be discussing exactly how you can produce an interesting and often inspiring story in just 500 carefully chosen words.

But of more immediate importance is finding out just what's in it for you.

What income can be expected?

Different systems

I began by writing advertising features for one newspaper group in North Wales and, after a few months' experience, applied for the same work with another group. Perhaps a little naïvely, I wasn't too concerned with how much money was involved. Initially I thought £30 or £40 a month would be ample reward for writing one or two features.

As it turned out, a high month can bring in as much as £1,200, a comfortable average being something over £500. And this work-load still allows me to plan my own work schedules, and leaves plenty of time for writing magazine articles, short stories and novels.

Occasionally, I manage to rest.

The system of payment usually takes the form of:

● A payment for lineage, perhaps a flat rate per hundred published lines (£12.50) and extra payment for each additional word (£0.101).
● A car mileage payment (£0.125 per mile).
● A refund of all telephone costs.

The examples given are for one of the newspaper groups. That particular group asks for a detailed claim on its pre-printed forms at the end of each month, listing the newspaper the feature appeared in, date, page number, mileage, phone costs, lineage, and grand total.

Comparable payments from the other newspaper group are based on a sliding scale of fees ranging from £16.50 for 400 words to

£31.00 for 750, plus £0.20 per mile car allowance, and all phone costs.

That second group clearly pays more, and monthly claims submitted need simply state the number of words written for each feature, and the costs incurred. Far less time-consuming.

Gross payments per feature averaged out for each newspaper group currently work out at £20.00 for group one, and £25.00 for group two (pay increases are rare). So from those figures it can be seen that to earn an average of £500 per month it's necessary to complete 25 features for newspaper group one, or 20 features for newspaper group two – between 4.5 and 5.5 features each week.

Overworked, underpaid?

What exactly does an average of five features a week mean in terms of time?

Five features means five businesses to be visited. So I set aside a complete working day for interviews. Features vary in difficulty, but generally I can comfortably produce 600 words of finished copy – from my own notes – in one hour. That makes a total of one working day interviewing, plus five hours writing time. A total of thirteen hours a week, for £500 a month.

Obviously, there are snags.

You arrange an interview, and when you get there the client is out. Or you can't arrange all the interviews for the same day, which means the five you have scheduled turn out to be spread over two or even three days. Nevertheless, even when all minor and major irritations are taken into account, you are – in my opinion – getting suprisingly well paid for stimulating part-time work.

Getting paid, moreover, for thirteen hours a week during which you are practising, and perfecting, the craft of writing.

Who needs advertising features?

Any business, small or large, anywhere.

Typical examples would be:

- The man making beautiful lutes and guitars in a back room of his home.
- The young woman embarking on a soft furnishing business in quaint premises on a busy street.
- The motor mechanic about to leave his/her job and become an independent businessman working from a Bedford Rascal.
- The double-glazing company moving to premises on a modern industrial estate.
- The multi-million pound international company keen to promote its environmentally friendly production methods.

In addition, you will frequently be called upon to write features advertising various functions or pointing the general public towards new facilities or forthcoming events. These can range from May Day parades and carnivals to agricultural shows, wedding 'fayres', swimming galas, new shopping malls, pantomimes – indeed, anything at all that the people involved decide will benefit from advance publicity.

What all these businesses, functions and events have in common is the desire to present their wares, their image, their message, to a public that often is only vaguely aware that they exist. They could achieve that aim by taking out their own full-page advertisement, but that can be expensive. In the case of the smaller businesses unlikely to have the writing skills essential for the message to be presented effectively, they will need to pay a PR company or advertising agency to write the text. An advertising feature is the ideal alternative.

When an advertising feature is arranged, the newspaper provides the space at no cost (or minimal cost if they are short on support ads). It designs the layout in close consultation with the client (this can include company logos), and fills it with professional photographs and well-written text that has been approved by the client.

Most important of all, the published feature will be read by people who live locally, and who do their purchasing or use services within the catchment area.

Where do features appear?

It follows from the previous paragraph that it would be pointless to have typical advertising features in a national newspaper. You will certainly find them in the familiar local newspapers that are delivered free, or sold for a few pence in local newsagents. Those newspapers will usually have a readership approaching or surpassing 20,000.

If you read your local newspaper, you will have skimmed through a lot of advertising features over the years. Many will have been of no interest to you. Others will have caught your attention because they happen to be dealing in goods or services you were in need of at that time – or because you know the people involved. And it's that fundamental parochial character that makes the local newspaper the ideal medium for an advertising feature.

What newspaper staff are involved?

The newspaper's advertising department will have telesales staff who are constantly selling advertising space to local businesses. Representatives will visit prospective clients, explain the way an advertising feature is organised, and get that vital list of suppliers who – it's hoped – will lend their support by taking out box ads.

Once all parties are in agreement, the features editor will brief the writer and photographer and they will arrange a suitable date for an interview, or photographic session. When the text has been written and delivered to the office, the features editor will give it the once over, ensure that the final version has been approved by the client, then pass it to the sub-editor for final shaping into the way it will appear on the page.

This final editing may well involve cuts, of which more later.

Who writes the feature?

Usually, the freelance correspondent. And that means you.

Editors know their staff reporters are busy chasing hard news, and they don't want to see them tied up for several hours throughout the week making appointments, interviewing, and writing advertising copy. The freelance correspondent is expected to be flexible. Appointments are often awkward to arrange – most proprietors like you to believe their business will collapse if they are away for more than five minutes – and are sometimes broken.

There is often poor communication between a newspaper's advertising and editorial departments. This means that you will frequently have last-minute emergency features thrown at you, with an interview to be arranged and copy delivered, all within a few hours. And while staff reporters stop work at a set time each day, you will often be sitting at your desk late into the evening.

In times of recession, different policies can be adopted. Towards the end of last year, one of the groups I worked for retrenched and, despite the inconvenience, turned all advertising features over to staff reporters. I'm expecting them to come back to me any day now. Because with a 500-word, well-crafted feature, a good, freelance advertising writer can work miracles for a struggling business.

And that's a skill that all editors appreciate.

2

HOW TO BREAK IN

If, as we've seen in the previous chapter, an editor values the skills of a good advertising feature writer, how easy is it to get work?

We've already established that the pay is acceptable, and that the hours seem reasonable. But what's the relationship between a freelance and the newspaper? Will there always be work there for you? Can you expect to be treated fairly, and not asked to work to impossible deadlines that expired sometime yesterday?

You have probably already marked your place in this book and hunted around for your local paper, there to study an advertising feature. You will have decided that, yes, this is for you – or no, you couldn't write like that for love nor money. My own belief is that, if you are dedicated to writing, at the very least your interest will have been aroused. This is a way to get into print, and make money; an opportunity that's very difficult to refuse. So you'll be looking for the answer to the above questions, and also wondering how you learn this craft, and where you go to get the job.

In this chapter you'll get the answer to some of those questions, an insight into typical working methods, and important advice on how to apply for the job.

We'll be looking at:

- What basic experience/writing skills are needed?
- Typical working routine.
- Is expensive equipment essential?
- Learning by studying published features.
- Trying your hand, using a real/imaginary business.
- Assessing your performance.
- Applying for the job.

12

What basic experience/writing skills are needed?

Unpublished, but unbowed

That, in a nutshell, is the lot of many of today's budding writers.

Not only has the whole literary scene changed, with publishing buy-outs and take-overs of long-established houses, and new magazines disappearing after one issue – but with jobs of any kind difficult to come by, more and more people are trying their hand at writing. It seems an easy option, whereas of course writing can be one of the most frustrating occupations imaginable.

It always has been. But now, to compound the problems, competition is more intense and the available slots for our works of literary excellence are daily diminishing. All of which seems to be implying that if you are an unpublished writer, there is little hope of success.

But whatever you do, don't despair.

I've already mentioned that most people embarking on a freelance writing career begin by penning articles or short stories for national magazines. You may have done that in the past. I hope you continue to submit your work. You will always be competing with the professionals, but good writing will inevitably find a home – yes, even in today's gloomy climate.

Track record

In the meantime, what you want is immediate, guaranteed success. You want commissions for your work for which payment is assured, and that exhilarating confidence boost that comes from seeing your work in print.

I can think of no surer way of achieving that aim than by applying for work as a freelance correspondent with your local newspaper. And you can apply with confidence, even if your experience to date is minimal, your list of published work non-existent. Yes, it does help if you have some sort of track record. But the nature of the work you are applying for doesn't require a

13

background which includes writing 400-page blockbusters for a major publishing house.

A long time ago, a wise man told me to remember the acronym KISS – Keep It Simple, Stupid. He was talking about salesmanship. Transmogrified to apply to our craft, it means you're certain to have odd bits of writing lying about that will serve you well as a reference.

When you look back through your files you may remember you wrote an interesting article on gardening for your parish magazine. A well-written letter of yours may have appeared in a local or national newspaper or a glossy magazine. If you are a graduate, you may have a copy of the hefty thesis you wrote for your degree.

All of the above constitutes a track record. Because although the term is usually taken to mean published work, for the purpose of applying for this job you merely need examples of your work. Published or unpublished. You need to show that you can get words down on paper. (If you really haven't got anything worth presenting, don't worry. Later on in this chapter I'll show you how to produce your first advertising feature, which you can confidently send with your job application or in answer to an editor's telephone request.)

Never discount old articles or stories that have been rejected by publishers. An editor is supposed to work objectively, with the interests of the particular publication always in mind. But acceptance of an article or story is always to a great extent subjective, and excellent pieces are often turned down simply because they don't strike a chord. If you are confident that a rejected piece you have put to one side fairly reflects your writing ability, then take it out of the bottom drawer, dust it off, and look at it with a critical eye. Even if it's a piece you wouldn't normally consider presenting with a job application, close examination may reveal merit that had previously gone unnoticed.

A command of English

You are not looking for talent. In this job you need to be a journeyman not a genius. What you are looking for is clarity. Do you see evidence of that, of an ability to put your thoughts down so that a reader – any reader – will know exactly what you mean? Do you write easily understood, uncomplicated sentences, and arrange them in logically constructed paragraphs, complete in themselves? Can you see a reasonable facility with words? Remember, when writing for the newspapers, you will always be thinking 'simple'.

Are you able to compose a body of text with a clearly defined structure – beginning, middle, end? Are you familiar with the rudiments of English grammar?

In other words are you, at the very least, a competent writer? If you answer no to any of the above questions, then it's not the end of the world but it does mean you will have difficulty making the grade. Put bluntly, if you have doubts about your basic writing ability, then be honest with yourself and proceed no further.

If you *can* string words together so that the end result is writing that can be understood by the average reader of a newspaper, then you have an adequate command of basic English. And to make a start writing advertising features, that's all the experience you need.

Typical working routine

Deadlines

All writing takes time. If you have been writing as a hobby then, typically, you will have grown accustomed to sitting down for an hour or so during the evening. But the time we're considering here is not the ample time you would like to have at your disposal so that you can write at leisure, but the hours or minutes you will actually have available to write each commissioned advertising feature.

I've already talked about the newspaper staff involved in the production of an advertising feature. All of them will be exceptionally busy, and they will expect your work to move along the line and arrive on their desk in time to meet their particular deadlines. As a freelance the only person you are likely to have contact with is the features editor, and he or she will set the time on a certain day of the week when your work must be ready. That's the deadline you must work to.

Let me give you an example from my own work.

The newspaper group I work for produces three papers of concern to me, two coming out on Thursday, one on Friday. The intricacies of production demand that the writer gets his work in early (the photographer has more time). So my copy is expected at the office on the Wednesday of the preceding week – eight days before print day.

This is not graven in stone. I know that at a push I can get away with submitting copy as late as midday Friday. But usually that's at the newspaper's pleasure, not mine. In other words, I would be loath to tell the paper that my copy was likely to be late, whereas the paper has no qualms about tossing me an emergency feature on Thursday and setting a revised deadline for midday Friday.

It suits them, so that's all right.

Work time

Advertising features are sold to clients well in advance, and the briefs – details of what's required – will come to you willy-nilly.

My own system for organising work is based on a Monthly Work Sheet I devised (there is a sample in the Appendix), which gets filled in as work is passed to me by the features editor. At the time of writing I have twelve features listed, some of which are not due in for another three weeks. There are times when I will have the details for features that are not due for three months.

Nevertheless, like most writers, I tend to leave the writing of each feature until the last possible moment. I do interviews on Tuesdays, and write four or five features on a Wednesday morning even if it means getting up at 5.00 a.m. Not a good system. And it certainly wouldn't be possible if I didn't know exactly how many words I can write each hour, without fail. I shudder to think what will happen when the word processor breaks down.

My advice to you is to begin as I began. Write each 500-word feature as soon after you have interviewed the client as possible. Read through several times. Rewrite. Revise carefully. At first you will be painfully slow. But as your list of published features grows you will find that you are getting into the swing of things and writing much more quickly.

When you reach that stage, you must make a firm commitment to balance speed with quality. It's no use dashing off a feature in thirty minutes if nothing you have written makes any sense. Nor is it going to help you earn money if you labour over every feature as if it were an entry for the Ian St James short story awards. If you want to advance at your chosen occupation you need to convince your editor that you can write as many advertising features as he/she cares to give you (within reason), and always deliver them at the appointed hour.

So for your own benefit you must attain a writing speed that is comfortable and enables you to write at your best, but is still fast enough to produce well-written features with considerable rapidity. From this optimum writing time you have arrived at you will be able to organise your work so that you constantly meet all-important deadlines. Those deadlines can loom threateningly when you are given an emergency feature. And at times like that, the tools you are using can be of immense help.

Is expensive equipment essential?

Pen versus word processor

The simple answer to the question is, no, it isn't. And it's an obvious answer, really, because the business of writing advertising features – or anything else for that matter – goes back to a time when quill pens were scratching away on sheets of luxurious vellum.

If I cast my mind back just five years I, too, can remember tapping out short stories and articles on an old Olivetti portable, crossing out and amending, physically cutting and pasting, and typing at least three drafts of everything I wrote. Yet many writers who once used a typewriter now insist they couldn't manage without their computer. I tend to agree with them, and not only because it reduces repetitive work. I firmly believe the computer makes writing more enjoyable and actually helps you to improve the finished product.

The most you actually need to complete your work satisfactorily is a typewriter and some bond paper and that's only essential for the final copy you send to the newspaper. If you are comfortable doing preliminary work using a pencil, fountain pen, rollerball or fibre-tip, then by all means continue to write that way. Many writers aver that a fountain pen forces them to write more slowly, thus preventing them from scribbling madly away, far ahead of their thoughts. I believe they have a valid point.

If you do decide to invest in a computer (and I honestly feel you should once you have a few months' feature writing under your belt), then don't make the mistake of assuming you need to lay out £1000 or even more. The Amstrad PCWs are sneered at by IBM compatible or Apple Mac owners, but I have been using their most basic model with complete satisfaction for the past four years.

Something like £500 will get you everything you need, including a printer. The latest models use 3.5in. disks, which are an industry standard. You will need a powerful, fully functional word processor with many features such as: being fast at leaping backwards and forwards through a document – something you will find yourself doing constantly – and performing a word count at a good rate of knots. It should also allow users to have two documents in memory at the same time, and switch blocks of text from one to the other.

Buy one with an efficient spell checker. Though I am old-fashioned enough to believe that some tasks should be left to the little grey cells, a good spell-check programme helps to pick out literals (typing errors). Conversely, it's of no use at all for locating the wrong use of words such as *there* and *their*, *to* and *too*, or *where* and *were*, for which you will need a grammar check.

What a computer does do for you is allow you to compose merrily on screen, altering constantly until you have the final version when you can print off as many perfect copies as you need. When you have a programme that allows you to edit a second document while the first is printing, then the time saved is considerable.

A modem (a device for transmitting from one computer to another, using telephone lines) and communications software are seldom needed. Fax machines can be extremely useful, and new or second-hand prices are now quite low. An answering-machine is almost indispensable. I will be talking towards the end of this chapter about always being available for work; an answering-machine ensures that you are, as do those convenient mobile phones.

One final plus point for word processors. Advertising features often get delayed by the client, or the newspaper, the copy put to one side and lost. If you are asked to produce a second copy a month after you wrote the first, your computer will oblige, every time, and with no effort on your part.

Learning by studying published features

Basic study

The wonderful thing about writing of any kind is that there is always plenty of study material available. We are going to be dealing with the nuts and bolts of advertising feature writing in great detail in Chapter 6 but, because it's absolutely no use applying for a job if you're not familiar with the finished product, some basic study is essential. Also, by examining published features – and by doing other simple research – you will be able to produce a 500-word feature of your own, modelled on those published examples, which will come in very useful.

The first thing to do is obtain some copies of your local newspaper, turn to the advertising features, and read through them several times.

You will probably find features advertising a selection of businesses – a pub, a restaurant, a garage – and you must note carefully the way the writers have treated each one. Look at the various bits of information the writer has included, where in the feature they have been placed, and their relevance and importance to the business being advertised.

See how much direct speech has been included (spoken comments by the owner or manager of the business), and how it affects the feature. Does it improve it, spoil it? Has it been done smoothly, or does it jar? Note the choice of words. Are there any you don't understand, at once? Is it written in the first person? And if not, how?

Finally, study the general structure and the particular way the writer has opened and closed. See if you can see some relationship or link between the beginning, and the end. Does the one lead in smoothly, does the other leave you with a feeling of completion?

It often helps to get the feel of an article or story by writing it out yourself from beginning to end. If possible use a typewriter, and try it with several features, ensuring that each takes up one side of an A4 sheet of paper. (See *Shuffle the pile*.) If you do this often enough, your subconscious will gradually become familiar with that style of writing – which is exactly what you want.

Study along these lines is invaluable, and will quickly give you a good understanding of the way an advertising feature is written. But before you can sit down with pen and paper and attempt to write your first feature, you will need a few facts.

Trying your hand using a real/imaginary business

Facts, plus imagination

The easiest way to simulate the research necessary for the production of an effective advertising feature is to choose a local business with which you are familiar, write down everything you know about it, and make up the rest.

Let's say you regularly use your local delicatessen.

You probably know the name of the proprietors, how long they have owned the business, the number of staff they employ and if they work full- or part-time. You certainly know the shop's location, its appearance and layout, the goods stocked, and the opening hours. What you are unlikely to know is what the proprietors did before they bought the delicatessen, what particular qualifications they have, their aims when they moved in, and their plans for the future.

It's that kind of information that you are going to have to invent. You want to make this little exercise as close to the real thing as possible. So take a shorthand notebook, jot down all the personal facts (Bert and Mabel Deli, moved in two years ago); a brief description of the shop (well laid out, two cold counters, fully tiled walls); add the invented bits (owned three previous shops, offer old-fashioned personal service, confidently expect to establish a successful chain); and complete with anything else you think might help you to write an advertising feature commissioned by the features editor of your local paper.

What you'll end up with is some scribbled pages in your notebook that will look very much like notes jotted down at an interview. You are all ready to go.

Now, it's very easy at this stage to select a published feature from those you've been studying that actually advertised a similar business. All you need do is change the names, slot in bits of information pertaining to your delicatessen, and you've got a ready-made advertising feature.

What I want you to do is take a last look at those published features, then put them firmly to one side and write your own feature, from scratch, using the notes you have assembled. If you like, you can time your work. But attach no importance to the time taken, for you will certainly have laboured over this first effort.

So far I've given you no writing instruction, quite deliberately, because I know you will be interested to see how you fare working from scratch. But you have already done some studying, and you will have retained a clear mental picture of the features you have read. My guess is you'll produce 500 words that are surprisingly professional, and it's quite easy to judge your performance.

Assessing your performance

Shuffle the pile

Earlier in this chapter I suggested you write or type several published advertising features, in order to familiarise your brain with their particular format and the style of writing. You'll remember I also suggested you finish up with several features on separate A4 pages.

Turn back to those now, slip your own carefully composed feature in amongst them, and shuffle well. Now read through the lot, and I'll warrant that you will be pleasantly surprised. You may not have produced a feature indistinguishable from the rest – nor should you, for you will have your own style. But if you've studied diligently and put your heart and soul into your writing you will certainly have produced a creditable first effort.

It could well be that this first effort, or the second, or perhaps the third, is going to secure for you that freelance position with your local paper.

Applying for the job

Letter or phone

The best answer to that is to quote some more examples from my own experiences.

I got my first job as advertising feature writer by replying to an advertisement. I did so by phone. When I had gained some experience, I applied for a similar position with the second newspaper group. Again, I approached them by phone, but this time it was 'cold'. I simply told them who I worked for, the job I was doing, how long I'd been employed, and asked if they needed a freelance. They did.

To secure the first job, I sent off two or three samples of work. For the second job, it wasn't necessary.

Let me say at once that I dislike query letters of any kind. Many magazines ask for article ideas to be submitted by post, yet I find that a telephone call always gets an answer, a query letter rarely so. This is not to criticise. Letters get lost in piles of other letters. A phone call is immediate and invites conversation or a simple yes or no.

So my strong recommendation is to approach your local news-paper by telephone. I would only advise against it if you feel your telephone voice is not all it should be. If you are not a good speaker, then write a letter.

Prepare, prepare...

The telephone call first.

If you choose this method of approach, first write down a rough draft of what you intend to say and make sure you have it to hand. If you have had work published, make a note of the titles, and where and when the articles or stories appeared. English qualifi-cations obtained at school or university can help if you are unpublished, so list any A levels, degrees, or other certificates.

It can be an advantage to have worked with people. Interview-ing work is particularly relevant, even if it was simple market research. It's also helpful if you can make an immediate start – it's surprising how newspapers often appear to have been waiting for your call. When you make the call, ask for the features editor in person. You can get his or her name from the switchboard. As soon as you are connected, introduce yourself and state clearly the purpose of your call. What you say might go something like this:

> 'Good morning Mr Adsed. My name is John Novice, and I'm interested in writing advertising features for the *Weekly Smudge*. Do you have any freelance work of that kind available?'

Unless you've caught the editor at a particularly busy time, you will almost certainly get a carefully considered response. If the newspaper uses freelance writers, then good ones are rarely turned away out of hand. Even if there is little work available at that time, the editor knows he must have reliable writers he can fall back on if regular freelances are ill, or on holiday. So at the very least he's probably considering trying you.

When compiling your crib sheet you will have anticipated ques-tions, and prepared your answers. Those most likely to be thrown at you will be the obvious ones:

23

- Are you a graduate?
- Have you any newspaper experience?
- How long have you been writing?
- What kind of work have you done?
- If I need you, how soon can you start?

You may be asked to send in samples of your work and I would suggest that if the conversation progresses that far, your chances are good. Send your best pieces (and you should certainly include the feature you wrote as an exercise), with a covering letter that confirms your enthusiasm, and your willingness to start at once.

Write yourself into a job

A written application has the advantage of demonstrating to the editor that you can put words on paper. Use the opportunity not only to list your qualifications and special attributes and inform the editor how keen you are to work for the paper, but to show him your neat, uncluttered prose, your command of words, your ability to get the maximum information across economically.

If there are several newspapers in your area, by all means apply to them all. But don't send carbon copies of your original letter. Retype, or print a fresh copy of the original letter for each application (and don't forget to change the names).

I had no problems working for the two North Wales groups. Their areas overlapped marginally, but both editors knew that I was employed by the competition, and had no objections. More than once I found myself writing a feature on the same establishment for both groups, though at different times. Needless to say, writing the feature the second time involved very little work.

A trickle to a flood

Looking back through my files, I see that I began writing advertising features in January 1990, and wrote three that first month. All of them were completed in the first week. On pay day I received, I believe, a cheque for £40. For July, 1991, I have no record of the number of features written, but that month my earnings from advertising features alone were £1,350. So in eighteen months, what began as a trickle swelled into a flood.

There are several factors which have a bearing on success or failure. I firmly believe that always being available and always meeting deadlines are very high on the list.

Most people – not all, but most – can be taught to write advertising features. But once you have learned the craft, developed the flair, call it what you will, you must be prepared not only to write features that come to you with an easily achievable deadline, but you must always meet that deadline, and you must put yourself out for your editor when emergencies arise.

You will be well rewarded.

One thing I haven't mentioned so far is that the work is to some extent seasonal. Firms tend not to advertise when they are at the end of their financial year. There is always a lull just after Christmas. On the other hand, summer is a wonderful time for wedding 'fayres', carnivals, seaside entertainment, local tennis tournaments, flower shows, agricultural shows etc. And in the two months leading up to Christmas there are parties and pantomimes, pubs and restaurants clamouring for custom, town centres being decorated, carol services. . .

If you have made yourself available in times of emergency, and put in those extra hours churning out a feature passed to you by a harassed editor, then your reward will be a flood of commissions during the bonanza times.

So leave your answering-machine on, and make yourself available. But before that, of course, you need to get your first professional assignment under your belt.

3

HANDLING YOUR FIRST ASSIGNMENT

With a clear picture in your mind of what constitutes an advertising feature, and a knowledge of what skills are required to write one, you are now ready to start work as a professional writer. So from this point onwards I will assume that you are in touch with an editor, or are through the negotiation stage and about to embark on your new career.

Neil Armstrong was in no doubts about the importance of his first step and, though you're not about to walk on the surface of the moon, you will certainly be treading strange ground. So a map is all important, and what this chapter will do is take you through the initial stages of advertising feature production – the work you must put in before you get down to the actual writing.

We will be discussing:

- A typical commission.
- Why a personal interview with a client is always best.
- Arranging the appointment.
- How much time to allow.
- What to take with you.
- Dress, attitude.
- Keeping in touch with your newspaper.

A typical commission

Your first assignment will almost certainly come to you by a telephone call from the features editor, or possibly from a member of the advertising staff. Typically, you will be asked if you are available to write the feature. (At which exciting moment you spill

26

your coffee, and answer in an inaudible croak.) You will then get details of the feature, given at breakneck speed so that if you haven't got shorthand or you own method of speed writing you will be making a mental note to learn – and quickly.

The information you get will be along these lines:

- Name, address and telephone number of the client or business.
- The name of the person you will be meeting.
- The reason for the feature. (New business, existing business recently refurbished or about to expand, etc...)
- The size of the feature. (More about this below.)
- The date the feature is required – your first deadline.
- Possibly some tips: client is going on holiday, phone immediately; be certain to mention the client's wife/husband; this one's awkward, tread carefully; and so on...

Everything in that list is straightforward, except the size of the feature. You may simply be told the number of words required, in which case, fine. Up to now I've talked about features being 500 words long, which is the way I think of them. But newspapers tend to look at them in 'column centimetres'.

So you might be told your feature has been allocated twelve centimetres times four columns – a total of forty-eight column centimetres – and for that to make sense you will need to know how many words fit into a single column centimetre in your particular newspaper.

If you measure one of the features you used for studying, you will probably find a column centimetre contains about twelve words. That means forty-eight column centimetres is the equivalent of 576 words, and you should now enter this figure on your Feature Work Sheet (you will find a sample at the end of the Appendix) together with all the other bits of information. The Feature Work Sheet also has a space for notes, which I find useful because my own jottings on loose bits of paper always get lost.

Why a personal interview is always best

Sometimes it's impossible to get face-to-face with your client. This usually happens when busy clients have proved so difficult to track down that when you do talk to them on the phone, your deadline is only hours away. But a personal interview is always what you should aim for, because no matter how skilled you are at extracting information from someone over the phone, you are dealing only with words.

Your client will merely answer your questions, only rarely volunteering interesting snippets of information. If you ask for a description of their premises, you will get a jaded/wildly imaginative, subjective viewpoint which may well leave out a vital feature that could bring your story to life. And because the telephone gives users the feeling of being pushed for time, some questions won't be asked, others will go unanswered – and what you do get down will be in your own, unreadable scrawl.

On the other hand, when you visit a business you will 'see' it with all five senses (even if the 'taste' is only a welcome cup of coffee). And you will be able to draw on each one of the vivid impressions you gained when you begin to paint your word picture.

Arranging the appointment

The first thing to remember when telephoning a client for an information-gathering appointment is that much of the hard work has already been done. Selling by telephone is very difficult. Most of the time, the salesperson is trying to convince a total stranger that he or she should buy something not wanted or needed.

You're not selling. The telesales staff at your newspaper have already overcome that hurdle and, by the time you are commissioned to write the feature, they will have visited the client to discuss layout, costs, support advertisements, and the date the feature will appear. In other words, they have broken the ice. The clients have seen roughs of what their advertising feature will look like, and they are now eagerly looking forward to seeing their business featured in the local newspaper. They are waiting for your call.

When you sit at your desk, pen poised, remember that some businesses start at 8.00a.m, others at 9.00a.m, shops at 9.30a.m and sometimes even 10.00a.m. It's also worth giving people time to hang up their coats and sort through the morning's mail.

Because of the information you have been given, when you

telephone you are able to ask for your client by name – always a good point. The switchboard or receptionist will certainly ask who's calling, and the simple reply is, 'John Novice, from the *Weekly Smudge*'.

Even though I'm not a member of staff, I find nothing wrong with introducing myself that way as I always explain later that I am a freelance writer. As an alternative, you could say, 'John Novice on behalf of the *Weekly Smudge*', but it really doesn't matter how you introduce yourself as long as you include your name, and the name of the newspaper.

You will need to explain why you want to see the client, because quite often there will be some confusion. The busy client will have forgotten all about the feature. Or there will be two features planned for the same business in rival newspapers. And sometimes the advertising people have been so vague that the clients don't even realise to what they've agreed.

Another problem you will come across is that the client will assume you are a member of the newspaper's staff, and will ask questions that are not your concern. How are the support advertisements going? If I don't get enough support, how much will the feature cost? Is the photographer coming, because all our vans are out today?

In all cases, listen, be polite, explain again who you are and why you want to see them, and suggest a day and time.

You will also be asked how long you're going to be there (because they are always very busy), and I would suggest you allow yourself at least thirty minutes for face-to-face talking.

Finally, if you're not familiar with the area, find out from the client how to get to the business address, and jot this information in the notes section of your Feature Work Sheet.

How much time to allow

This is something like the old question, how long is a piece of string? It's got a little bit to do with how long you are going to be face-to-face with your client, but when you have a list of appointments to fit into the same day, you must also give some thought to possible complications.

In a perfect world, you'd drive to the business, talk to the client over a cup of coffee and drive away.

What can happen is you get stuck in traffic, and you're fifteen minutes late. Because of this, the client must keep you waiting, as an important meeting has started. When you do see the client, there are constant interruptions. (I often find myself interviewing in a busy shop, in front of customers.) Or the client can talk the hind leg off a donkey... Or won't talk at all, and you must start probing... Or – and this often happens – no matter how hard you dig there really is very little information at all, and you know you're going to have to write an imaginative piece of fiction.

Obviously, you can't allow for every possible eventuality, so you must weigh up the travelling involved, add a little bit for traffic delays and unforseen problems at the interview – and arrive at a realistic figure and hope for the best. After all, if the worst comes to the worst you can always ask the client if you can use the phone to put back your next appointment.

What to take with you

- A shorthand notebook.
- Two pens.
- A tape recorder, spare batteries and cassettes.
- A diary.
- Copies of previous features promoting the business.

You will have your own personal preferences.

I use a shorthand pad but because they're reversible I often find myself getting lost and starting on the wrong page. Some people like to use a clipboard holding a lined A4 pad. This provides a portable work surface and makes life easier when you are jotting notes as you walk through a factory or workshop, or around the outdoor displays at a garden centre.

Ball pens, fibre-tips, rollerballs – all are better than fountain or cartridge pens, which don't dry quickly enough. A tape recorder is never as good as written notes (my opinion), but is often useful as back-up. But it has the disadvantage of making some clients nervous, and in those cases should never be used. The diary will contain details of all your appointments. You need it with you because there will be times when you don't even get past reception. The client has been called away, but wants you to arrange another appointment.

Copies of previous articles featuring the business are always useful. At the outset, you can get them from the newspaper's files. After about six months you will find that you are returning to businesses you have already visited, and written about. So make a habit of keeping all features on disk if you have a computer, or typing an original plus carbon copy. (I used to cut out all my published features, stick them to A4 sheets and file them in clear plastic covers.)

Seeing the previous feature always jogs the client's memory. In modern jargon, I suppose it takes them out of their business administration mode and into feature-writing mode. Whatever you call it, it helps them to divulge information, give interesting quotations, generally breathe life into what can often be a fairly ordinary subject – their business.

Dress, attitude

Thomas Fuller said that, 'Good clothes open all doors', while according to Samuel Johnson, 'A man with a good coat upon his back meets with a better reception than he who has a bad one'.

Nowadays those sentiments might be thought of as old-fashioned. Yet as you go about your work as an advertising feature writer you will find that the male and female staff of your newspaper wear suits or smart clothes all year round, and you would be wise to conform. Your concern is not that the door should be opened to you but that, when it is, the reception you get is a good one. For nothing can be more frustrating than a client who won't co-operate.

Your attitude will have been clear to your clients from the moment you first spoke to them on the phone.

Politeness is essential, and you must also have a pleasant manner (even if you've got a hangover, or a heavy cold), and be the model of discretion. That means not talking about other businesses except in a most general way, not knocking opposition (other businesses, other newspapers), and certainly not acting in an underhand way.

It's important to remember that you are talking to people who believe you are some kind of a reporter. A reporter means horror stories about the tabloid press. And although your clients will understand that the *Weekly Smudge* is not exactly the depths of sleaze, they will still be wary of saying too much, or of having what they do say taken the wrong way. So you must also inspire confidence.

Always let your clients know when what they are saying will not be printed. For what it's worth, when something is obviously 'off the record', put your pen away, close your notebook. Never, never put anything into your feature that was told to you in confidence. If your clients give printed information to you (restaurant menus, beauty salon brochures, scrapbooks adding up to years of a golf club's history), find out if they want it back, and return it promptly.

Before you take your leave, let the client know exactly what is going to happen, when the feature will appear, what to do with the pre-publication copy you will send or deliver to them – and anything else over and above that pertaining to the *Weekly Smudge*. Because – as frequently happens to me – you may find a particular business so unusual that it immediately starts you thinking along the lines of a national magazine feature.

Keeping in touch with your newspaper

Although – at first – they will whisper not a word in your ear, feature editors can and do adjust deadlines. Nevertheless, it's always wise to treat the deadline you have been given as immutable. If anything occurs that looks like setting you back, let your editor know at once. Telephone, and explain the problem.

The most frequent impasse is caused by clients who don't keep appointments. Often this is because of a genuinely crowded schedule, and all you can do is keep trying. If the deadline is reached and you are still having no luck, the editor may suggest you do the interview over the phone. If that is clearly impracticable, you will be given a later deadline, and if that can't be met then the feature will be put back to a later date. Even then, you will know that at some time you are certain to come face to face with this particular client – and of course there are all those other clients whose appointments are drawing ever closer.

So the next thing you need is some basic knowledge of interviewing techniques.

INTERVIEWING TECHNIQUES

Interviewing techniques are infinitely varied, and must always be tailored to suit the occasion. Television and radio give prime examples. If you compare Jeremy Paxman's *Newsnight* manner with Sue Lawley's approach to her guests on *Desert Island Discs*, you are looking at extremes. Yet both techniques have been carefully honed to produce the desired result.

In Mr Paxman's case, he is hoping to drag information from – usually – politicians or important figures from industry or commerce for whom evading questions is an art form. Sue Lawley, on the other hand, is there to put nervous guests at ease and create a marvellously relaxed studio atmosphere.

Your brief – finding out all you can about a business in order to write an upbeat advertising feature – means that your aims are similar to those of the admirable Mr Paxman, although adopting the methods that work well for him would get you nowhere. You need to achieve his results, but by employing a technique closer to that used by Sue Lawley.

This chapter will attempt to show you how to succeed, by looking at:

● The importance of punctuality.
● The businesslike approach.
● Conducting/controlling the interview.
● Handling problem clients.
● Effective note-taking.
● The use of a tape recorder.
● Closing the interview.
● The problems/advantages of writing a feature from a telephone interview.

The importance of punctuality

Timekeeping is always important. If you've booked seats for *The Phantom of the Opera*, you don't want to slink into the theatre fifteen minutes after the curtain has gone up. Nor do you want to arrive at a bus stop at ten o'clock if the bus were due at nine forty-five. But there's an important difference between those examples, and arriving late for an interview with a client. In the first case, you'll still see most of the show, while in the second, well, there's usually another bus. But if you are late for an interview with clients, chances are they're no longer available. If they're very busy, it may be impossible to make another appointment, and that means a deadline missed, an advertising feature that doesn't get off the ground.

Even more important, your clients will almost certainly inform the newspaper that you had an appointment at such and such a time, but failed to arrive. Your reputation as a reliable feature writer will be in tatters.

If you've made an appointment, always be prepared to move mountains to get there on time. If you can't, then do telephone ahead, explain that you'll be late, and either ascertain that your clients will still be there, or make another appointment there and then.

One further point. A delayed appointment has a domino effect. Being late once means you've either got to scramble like mad to reach your other appointments on time, or make more apologetic phone calls.

The businesslike approach

My first appointment was on a rainy day when my car was off the road. I travelled by bus, got off at the nearest stop, arrived at a delightful pub with rainwater streaming from my waxed jacket, and throughout the interview my glasses persisted in steaming up.

But I presented myself in a businesslike manner.

We've already discussed the importance of dress. Of equal importance is the way you approach the business.

The way to do it is:

34

- Park in the customers' car park, not in an employee's personal space.
- Go to reception, announce yourself, and your business.
- If there is likely to be a wait, accept it, sit down, relax.
- When your client is available, again introduce yourself, shake hands, and wait to be invited to sit down.
- Be alert, attentive, note your surroundings, try to judge the type of person you are dealing with.
- But... if the delay drags on, don't wait too long. You, too, have a busy schedule.

All of this assumes that you are dealing with a small- to medium-sized business with office facilities and the staff to deal with visitors. But you will also be called upon to write about mechanics working in back-street garages, and your approach may involve bending down to peer under a car.

Yes, of course it makes a difference. It would be silly to announce yourself to the man lying flat on his back and covered in oil the way you would present yourself to an elegant receptionist. You will adjust your manner accordingly, introduce yourself in a more casual way, even crack a joke if you're good at that kind of thing (I'm not).

When you stand back and examine what you are doing, nothing changes. You parked well clear of the MOT bays. You announced yourself to the busy mechanic. You accepted his invitation to wait while he washed his hands (but in the MOT observation bay or draughty workshop, not a cosy reception foyer). And you kept your eyes and ears open when you went through to his office (if he had one) and accepted coffee from a chipped mug.

Conducting/controlling the interview

General points

Your clients will range from those who sit in total silence, appearing to be either exhausted or completely baffled, to others who slap four closely typed sheets of paper in front of you and tell you

35

airily that, 'the wife/husband has a wonderful way with words, you'll probably just need to print that as is'.

You must be able to deal with both these extremes, and all the shades of grey that come between them. And though you must never browbeat, you must always be in control.

The progress of an imaginary interview is followed in the next chapter, but it will help you to appreciate what goes on in if you are aware of certain fundamentals that govern dealings with people. Many of these principles were expounded by the American author and teacher, Dale Carnegie, but without doubt they were understood before he arrived on the scene and are in use now by people who have never read his books.

You must make your clients feel important, and one way of doing it is to remember their name, and to use it. But above all else, you must have an abiding interest in people, and the ability to talk in terms of your clients' interests. It's very easy to listen to what your clients are telling you, think of an incident from your own life that you feel is just as interesting, and spend the next few minutes telling them all about it. Do it sparingly, by all means; in that way, you are creating a pleasant, two-way conversation. But always return quickly to the matter in hand, and ask your next question.

At the beginning of the interview, your clients will probably sit down with you in a reasonably quiet place and say immediately, 'I've never done this kind of thing before'. Reassure them. Although by now they must know why you're there, tell them again, explain how many words the feature will contain, and explain that you will need a lot of information.

Make it quite clear that this feature is about their business. Let them know that you are going to write a story, but it's their story and you will need them to tell you what they want in it.

A logical progression

I usually begin an interview by asking clients why they decided they would like an advertising feature. Often they have no idea; the feature was probably sold to them by the newspaper's advertising staff. Nevertheless, I have taken a step forward, a two-way conversation has been initiated, and already I am talking to them in terms of their interests. Once they are talking freely to me (or not, in which case, see below), I then ask them to step into the past, and tell me why they started the business in the first place.

From there it's easy to move forward one step at a time, building up a complete word picture that concludes with their plans for the future. *Their* plans; *their* business; *their* future.

You must prompt them if they become stalled and at a loss for words. Listen to them if they digress, then gently bring them back on track. If you are interrupted, when the interview restarts, remind your client where you were up to, and continue. Sometimes there are constant interruptions. Asking clients if they would prefer you to come back at a more convenient time often makes them more aware of the problem. Occasionally, they will admit defeat and arrange to see you on another day.

If you are to have complete control of an interview, you need to have a clear picture in your mind of the way you want it to progress. Some preparation beforehand is helpful; just a few pencil notes showing a logical progression from the introduction to the conclusion.

Throughout, you will be prompting your clients with a series of questions, and the following are some you could put to them:

- Why did they start this particular business?
- What had they been involved in before? What qualifications or experience did they have?
- Is it a partnership, family business, limited company?
- Did they have a 'vision': a grand plan to create the perfect family pub, the most luxurious hotel, to dish up the fastest of fast foods?
- How did they go about it?
- What services or goods do they now provide or supply?
- What makes those services or goods different, or unique?
- Is there a particular reason for the feature? If not, is there some aspect of their business they wish to highlight?
- What about the future? What comes in the next year, or the next five years?

The answers to these basic questions will themselves lead you to more questions, and will start your clients thinking, and contributing unsolicited information. By following a similar pattern of question and answer (you will use some of the above, and others of your own that you find useful), you will usually come away with everything you need to know – if you also practise at being a good listener.

But even this admirable trait doesn't guarantee success.

Handling problem clients

As you grow in experience you will learn that there are frequently recurring interviewing problems caused by clients who fit into recognisable types. Among the problems you will face are:

- The client who talks about anything and everything, takes up valuable time – but gives you nothing of any use.
- The non-talker. Clients who give a succession of one-word answers to questions such as 'why did you start this particular business?' (Unemployed. Bored. Or just a baffled shrug.)
- 'Flowery prose' clients who want every word of what they've written – and mis-spelled – printed without change.
- Clients who think you have endless time to write and re-write, with each succeeding draft being submitted for their approval.

In some ways, talkative clients are preferable to those that contribute nothing without the use of an interrogator's crowbar. Despite the endless stream of words you will always find, amidst a lot of useless information, tiny specks of gold. Your job is to be selective; to pan for that gold like an old-time fossicker, while allowing the useless gravel to fall back into the verbal stream.

At the same time, you must be alert for comments that allow you to jump in with a pertinent question or remark that brings the client back on track.

For example, if you are interviewing a restaurant owner who rambles incessantly about his many, second-rate competitors and their ridiculous prices, you could interrupt by asking if he feels his establishment offers value for money and go on to discuss his menus. If he's a hotelier, ask if he believes people will always pay for quality, and let him extol the virtues of the luxurious wedding-suite. Clients who wander so far afield that they begin talking

38

about their holidays on the sunny Algarve can be brought back to the present by asking them if their trade is seasonal.

In other words, you let this kind of client talk about anything and everything, meanwhile listening attentively to see what can be turned around to suit your purpose: recording useful, relevant information for a feature about his or her business.

You must always be a good listener, but in different ways. When faced with talkative clients, you listen to select. On the other hand, with clients that seem at a loss for words you must listen when there is nothing being said.

I call it impregnating the pause. I simply ask a question, listen to the one-word answer, nod, and say nothing. Just smile, and wait.

Do this, and you will find that the silence becomes so strained that someone has to say something. It mustn't be you. What your clients eventually say out of desperation may have nothing to do with the original question. But because this type of person never indulges in small talk, it will almost certainly be of importance, and relate to the business.

Record this gem, and proceed.

Clients with a literary bent must be praised, and apprised. Admire their prose but tell them that, delightful though it is, it will need reshaping to conform with the newspaper's style. You will retain the essence of what they have written, you tell them, but carefully reword it for the average newspaper reader. From that comment your clients can infer what they will. Incidentally, some of these pieces are very well written, and in any case I always ask clients if they have put words to paper as it invariably reduces the need for close questioning.

One word of caution. In supplied copy there will usually be important information missing. Read carefully what your clients have written, and resort to your question-and-answer technique to make good any omissions.

Constant vetting of your work is usually suggested by managers of medium-sized businesses. They are either full of their own importance, or acting on the orders of their superior, who doesn't trust their judgment. You will always send clients a copy of your finished piece, so that they can correct inaccuracies before typesetting. Those who believe that constant rewriting is possible must be told that you have a deadline, it is graven in stone, and unfortunately it doesn't leave much time.

Effective note-taking

If you are able to control the interview to such an extent that it proceeds at your chosen pace, then taking notes is no problem. But clients are usually in some haste. You have other appointments looming and there is an awful lot of information to get down in the time available. Shorthand is ideal, if you are really competent. Other forms of speed writing will do equally well, and you may even have devised a method of your own.

The essentials are these. You need to get down every bit of information clients give you when they are aware that you are taking notes, and continue to jot down additional snippets of interest that come out in conversation. And everything must be readable. By you. Instantly. Because very often clients will ask you to read your notes back to them, so that they can get their bearings.

Although you have a set plan by which your interview continues on its logical way, your clients haven't seen the plan. They will jump backwards and forwards as ideas occur, so it's always a good plan to make your notes in paragraphs, with ample space between each one. That way, you can insert late information in its correct place, with no need to resort to asterisks and squiggly arrows pointing hither and thither.

Using a recorder

It's all too easy to assume that a recorder makes written notes unnecessary. I made this mistake when interviewing in the entrance hall of a technical college, and discovered – too late – that I had a wonderful recording of noisy students, but very little of the client's cultured tones. Background noise, and the ebb and flow of normal conversation, make a recording difficult to follow.

Even when it works well – a quiet room, a clear speaker, clients who don't mind a recorder standing on their desk – you will find that some words simpy fade away. And because a recorder isn't selective, you spend an awful lot of time in your office listening to the recording *and making notes from it*.

From this, you will have gathered that I don't like recorders. I

40

don't; with one exception, I never use them. However, quite often I have to do features about shopping in local towns. These are very popular at Christmas. To do them properly, I need to walk through the shopping-centre, making a note of all the shops on both sides of the road or in brightly lit malls. And although here, too, background noise is a nuisance, I do prefer a miniature recorder to making written notes on the move, sometimes while being buffeted by wind and rain.

I've got nothing against them as back-up. It's always possible that they will pick up a casual aside that you failed to note, and that one remark gives you a perfect lead, or close, for your story.

Closing the interview

You finish the interview when you have got everything you need to write a perfect feature. Already you will have an idea for an opening and, while listening to your clients, you will have been making mental notes on the way you will handle this particular piece. However, you must continue to think in your clients' interests and, before taking your leave, be sure to ask if there is anything at all that they want to add. If necessary, read your notes aloud, let them register, and wait. If nothing is forthcoming, then it's time to go.

Leave your clients fully informed. Let them know when they will receive their copy of the feature, how they can get in touch with the newspaper if they want to correct inaccuracies, and when the feature is due to be published.

On your way out, take another look around. Sit in your car, look back at the building. Take note of the surroundings; the business you are featuring is in a real world, and your readers want to enter that world.

The telephone interview – its problems and advantages

In my opinion, the main problem with a telephone interview is that you cannot do what was suggested in the last paragraph. Unless you are familiar with the area where the business is located,

41

and the business itself – the interior of the workshop or beauty salon, the craft items on display in a country cafeteria – you cannot describe it.

You must rely on the description that comes to you over the telephone, and it never works out quite as well. And if you come up against a problem client – talkative, reticent – then you must grip the receiver, grit your teeth, and be patient.

One essential for the telephone interview is a crib sheet. Make a list of your usual questions (as detailed above), but also try to 'get inside' the business before you pick up the receiver and dial. If it's a business dispensing a service, the surroundings are not so important. But make a note to ask who uses the services, their reactions to them, if they are private or business people. Is advertising effective? Is the business's trade local or national?

If you are telephoning a shop, the layout will be important. Remember to ask about shelves, cold counters, centre islands, lighting, colour, shop front, window displays – everything that would register automatically if you actually walked into the premises. And if you are dealing with a pub, find out where the dart board and pool tables are located, how the seating is upholstered, if the bar is panelled, what ornaments they have hanging from the oak beams, and if there is a beer garden and children's play area.

What are the advantages of a telephone interview? Well, there's no travelling involved, no builder's yards to walk through in the rain, no face-to-face confrontations that can result in personality clashes. It's also very easy to focus on each aspect of the business in turn. Interruptions are eliminated (though pub background music and chatter can be annoying), and both you and the client can concentrate.

Finally, it sometimes helps to make two phone calls. During the first, tell the clients the questions you are going to ask and give them an hour or so to come up with their answers. Then, at your second call, it's just a matter of filling in spaces.

5

A TYPICAL SMALL-BUSINESS INTERVIEW

With something like 2,000 interviews behind me, during which I've talked to the owners, proprietors, managers or directors of businesses ranging from Pilkington's Optronics Division to a cobbler's workshop in a garden shed, it's inevitable that a pattern should have emerged. By casting aside the extremes – the extremely easy and the extremely difficult – I have been able to come up with what I consider to be the typical interview.

Very few are straightforward, yet seldom are the difficulties insurmountable.

This 'typical' interview is presented to you in the form of a story written in the first person. The owners of the shop to be featured are Bert and Mabel Deli, the intrepid feature writer is John Novice and, of course, the newspaper is the *Weekly Smudge*. I had fun writing it, and for those of you who have never conducted an interview of any kind, I'm sure it will be enlightening.

The interview

It was already ten o'clock when I finished dealing with the mail and glanced at my watch, and I knew that if I was going to get to the Coleslaw Delicatessen by ten-thirty I'd have to hurry.

Quickly, I checked my briefcase – notebook, diary, feature worksheet, spare pen – switched on the answering-machine, and left. On the short drive across town I left the radio off and thought about the forthcoming interview. I knew the proprietors had only recently taken over the business, which meant the one previous feature the *Weekly Smudge* had offered as a guide would have

43

been useless. But that didn't bother me at all. I always prefer to work from scratch anyway, as I find rewriting somebody else's work very laborious.

The delicatessen was on the main road – number 54, Upper Down Street – so there was no chance of parking immediately outside. I drove past, found a parking space down the nearest side street, and walked into the bright little shop just before the half hour.

The man behind the counter glanced up, smiled, and said, 'Yes, sir?'

'Mr Deli?'

'That's me.'

'Good morning, Mr Deli. My name is John Novice, from the *Weekly Smudge*.'

'Oh, right,' Mr Deli said, smiling and extending his hand. 'You're here about that feature?'

'I certainly am, I – '

'Well,' he cut in, 'you're wasting your time, actually, because I gave all the details to that young woman from your office.'

'Ah.' I smiled, and shook my head. 'Some confusion, Mr Deli. What you gave her were instructions about your advertisement. What I'm here for is to get a great deal of information so I can write the editorial; the actual feature.'

'If it goes ahead.'

'Is there a problem?'

'Well, as far as I know we haven't had many replies from the people taking out support ads. And if that's the case... '

'Don't worry about it. If they're slow, the paper will put your feature back a week or so. But now that I'm here at least we can get the editorial side of things sorted out.'

He shrugged. 'O.K., if you say so. Would you like to come through?'

As he went behind the counter a dark-haired woman in an overall passed us.

'My wife, Mabel,' Mr Deli said. 'She'll see we're not disturbed.'

I smiled, said, 'Hello, Mrs Deli, lovely day,' then followed her husband through into a spotlessly clean preparation room with a central, marble-topped table and shelves stacked with dry goods.

He pushed some invoices to one side, pointed to a chair, then sat down alongside a scrubbed table that doubled as his desk.

'I'm not much good at this,' he said, frowning. 'I haven't got a clue what you want to know.'

'Straightforward, really. A bit of background information, and then the story of the Coleslaw Delicatessen. Is this your first business, Mr Deli?'

'Lord, no! We ran a café in Everybach for years, on Lower Down Street, but... ' He was watching as I got out my notebook and prepared to write. 'Do you really need to put that down?'

I shook my head. 'Not if you don't want me to. This is your feature, Mr Deli, and I'll write nothing without your approval.' I wrote the name of the shop at the top of a fresh page, then looked at him enquiringly. 'What if I just say you've been in the food business for most of your life? Would that be about right?'

'Absolutely. From the time I left school.'

'O.K. And Mrs Deli?'

'Only for the past few years. She had the kids to look after before that.'

'Right. Now then, you had a successful café – so why change direction and open a delicatessen?'

'Well, that's a good question!'

I smiled. 'Was it an existing business?'

'Not a food shop, no. It was ladies' fashions for years, till the owner retired.'

'So you obviously needed planning permission for change of use. You must have been pretty certain you were doing the right thing?'

Mr Deli nodded in the general direction of the street, his expression canny. 'You see any other delicatessens out there?'

I shook my head. 'There you are then. No competition at all... '

'So it was an empty premises, in just the right place,' I said, scribbling away, 'and you saw an obvious gap in the market?'

'Certainly. Obvious to me. Until we opened our own shop we had to drive three miles for top quality cold meats.'

'But now locals have your excellent shop, right on their doorstep. Has the reaction been good?'

Mr Deli raised his eyes. 'Unbelievable! It's quiet, now, but that's unusual. Usually you can't get through the door, and you should see it lunchtime when we open the sandwich bar.'

I nodded. 'Was that in the grand plan from the beginning?'

'Sandwiches?' He shook his head. 'Public demand, actually.

45

We started doing the odd sandwich for some office people across the road, and it snowballed.'

'Right, now, when did you actually take over, Mr Deli?'

'Oh, that'd be early August. But we didn't open for business until mid-September.'

The doorbell sounded, and I looked up from my pad and along the passage to see an elderly couple entering the shop.

'Two of your satisfied customers,' I said, and Mr Deli nodded.

'They seem to know just what they're looking for, and I certainly like the feel of the shop,' I said. 'Obviously all the fixtures and fittings are new but, in that month before you opened, did you design the layout, do all the structural and decorating work yourself?'

'No chance! That was a local builder, and I couldn't have gone to a better bloke.'

'Would you like to give him a mention?'

'Wouldn't leave him out. William Fixit, Builders. He was the main contractor, and then there was Sparks the electrician and U. Bend did all the plumbing... '

'O.K... Now then, I've got brief details of your background, and your reasons for opening the shop. But what about the dream? Because there's always a dream, isn't there? You know the sort of thing. What did you and Mabel have in mind when you thought of Coleslaw Deli? Establishing the best delicatessen in the area? The first of several? Or something more than that?'

Mr Deli pursed his lips. 'To stay small, and simple, provide old-fashioned, personal service, and quality,' he said carefully. 'You'll have a walk round after, will you?'

'Definitely. I need to describe the shop, the layout and so on.'

'Right, well you'll see that we've got a lot of top quality brands that people might not have heard of. Pickles made by a firm in Yorkshire. Jams and preserves by another down in Devon. The best, in my opinion, though not the best known.'

'Right, so how shall we put that? Can we say that you spend a lot of time travelling the country, seeking the very best for your customers – that about right?'

'And it's all healthy stuff,' he agreed, nodding. 'No artificial ingredients, preservatives. All top quality.'

'Fine. So let's just recap.' I turned back to the first page. 'You've been in food all your life and, after running a successful café, you and Mabel decided to open a delicatessen when you saw a gap in the market. Is it run as a partnership, by the way?'

'In all but name. I'm sole proprietor, but you can see for yourself I couldn't manage without Mabel.'

'Then I won't bother mentioning any status. I'll just say that Bert and Mabel Deli opened the Coleslaw Delicatessen with the intention of providing good, old-fashioned, personal service, and a range of high-quality goods unlikely to be found in the average grocer's shop. Anything to add to that before we take a walk around?'

'Our own pies, sausage rolls, quiches. We bake them all on the premises – well, Mabel does – and they're snapped up.'

'Sounds delicious!' I stood up, and glanced around. 'So, this is the preparation room cum office. And the kitchen's through there?'

Mr Deli went across and opened the door, and I gazed into a compact room with fully tiled walls, gleaming, stainless-steel fittings and large upright freezers.

'Mabel'll be coming through shortly, when I take over out there. And we've got a part-time assistant comes in at eleven. She'll help with lunchtime sandwiches and so on.'

'Anything about her?' I asked as we walked through into the shop. 'Well known locally, on any government scheme – anything at all?'

'She's in the local running club,' Mabel Deli said, handing change to a customer. 'June Swift. Best in her age group, something like that.'

'Member of Everybach Harriers,' I said. I wrote that down, smiling my thanks as she handed over to Bert and went off to start work in the kitchen.

The shop was empty again and I followed Bert Deli around as he pointed out various features.

'We keep all our teas behind the counter. See, there, those classy-looking tins. Then next to them there's the coffees – we sell ready packaged, or loose beans, and there's a grinder over there so customers can grind the beans themselves.'

'Right, and you've got two very long cold counters – an excellent range of cheeses, I see.'

'Absolutely. We specialise in British and Continental cheeses, already got a reputation for that, plus our homemade products – there in the other counter. And over here, this is the new sandwich bar. I had to put that in within two weeks of opening – ' He broke off, smiled at a slim young woman who'd just come in, and said, 'Hi, June, pop in and see Mabel, she wants a word before you start... '

'It's great,' I said, gazing at the displays. 'I particularly like those old signs – the Bisto Kids, and that one there, Family Grocer. They give the place that certain atmosphere... '

'Old-fashioned,' Bert Deli said. 'Synonymous with quality, or so people like to believe – though you and I know it's not always true, right?'

'No, but that's the image you're trying to create. Good, old-fashioned quality. A shop where any grandmother would feel at home – nostalgia, a loaf for a tanner, butter cut from a slab... '

'You've got it,' Bert Deli said. 'That image, but with modern methods of hygiene – and believe me, people love it.'

'I think we've got enough for a good story, Mr Deli. Unless you can think of anything we've missed. This feature is really to let people know you're here – but is there anything else you want to highlight, anything at all?'

The doorbell pinged as Bert Deli was deep in thought and young June the athlete came briskly through to serve her first customer of the day.

'I don't think so,' Bert Deli said. 'We've mentioned the image, and the only thing we can add is it's a family business – oh, yes, my daughter helps at weekends, her name's Deirdre – and then that's about it.'

'Now, today's Tuesday,' I said, packing away my notebook, 'and I'll have written this and handed it in to the paper by tomorrow midday. I'll send you a copy by Thursday morning, and if I've got anything totally wrong – names, dates, products, whatever – call the number on the top of the sheet, and let them know.'

'Fair enough,' Bert Deli said, nodding. 'And what about the photographer, when's he coming, d'you know?'

'Afraid not. But if the *Weekly Smudge* doesn't let you know quite soon, give them a ring. Oh, and phone those alterations through by midday Friday, otherwise it's too late.'

We shook hands again and, as I left the shop, I had a quick look at the window displays, the general design of the shop front, then headed for my car.

'A shop where any grandmother would feel at home...' I mused

48

as I drove away. Not a bad line to put somewhere near the beginning of Bert Deli's advertising feature.

Comments

A quick glance back at the list of suggested questions in the previous chapter will show that all of them were answered in this example of a typical interview. Conversely, not all of them were actually asked. Bert Deli himself told me that they would, '...stay small, and simple...' so there was no real need to discuss his plans for the future.

You will also have noticed that questions weren't put as if the subject (or victim) were sitting in front of a bright light. During the course of what was a pleasant conversation, many just happened to be the natural, logical thing to say. For example, when Bert spoke proudly of his new shop providing local people with cold meats, it was natural to ask if reaction had been good.

It was also logical to suggest that Bert must have know what he was doing when he converted a ladies' fashion shop into a delicatessen. And if he had run a café for 'many years' it was reasonable to assume it was successful, and an expression of genuine interest to ask about the reasons for switching to a delicatessen. But I didn't questions his reasons for not wanting the café mentioned. Because of experience – I'd seen it all before, and although many businesses feel they are unique, few actually are – I was able to suggest phrases that accurately described what Bert and Mabel were doing. One example was, '... spend a lot of time travelling the country, seeking the very best for their customers...' Or, '... after running a successful café, Bert and Mabel Deli decided to open the Coleslaw Delicatessen when they saw a gap in the market... ' And, of course, '... a shop where any grandmother would feel at home... '

Businesses of all kinds depend on goodwill. When there have been alterations, extensions, renovations, and tradesmen have been employed, most clients will want to mention their names. Often, they forget, so always ask about main contractors.

A closet novel is one that excludes the outside world. You don't want to write a 'closet feature', so do as I did, and ask if there's anything special about employees, assistants, even the clients themselves. People are interested when they learn that a shop assistant is a well-known local runner, a businessman regularly plays in Pro-am golf tournaments, or the local chimney sweep once got halfway up Everest.

Listen to what's being said, be alert for anything that can bring your story alive, and if, at the same time, you can see a connection between outside interests and the business being featured, so much the better. Who knows, perhaps June Swift discovered a small but noticeable improvement in her running performances when she began eating the fresh, wholesome foods provided by the Coleslaw Delicatessen?

6

WRITING – PLANNING AND PREPARATION

Before actually writing the feature from your own notes and recollections, other people's quotations, and the welter of ideas demanding to be set free, you will need to know what your finished piece of writing should look like, and how to scale that professional peak.

You have assiduously studied advertising features, and even written your own by recalling details of a local business familiar to you. But what you have not done is to examine the skeleton that lies beneath the flesh of every article, the nuts and bolts involved in creating it, and the way the finished article must not only capture the correct mood for the business you are advertising, but also conform with your newspaper's house style.

So this chapter is all-important. It deals with each of those issues, and will lead you smoothly and with confidence sky high into Chapter 7: Writing the feature.

Remember that while we all need a general pattern to which we must conform, the world is crying out for originality. If you can work within the fairly flexible boundaries that define what is and is not acceptable in advertising feature writing yet still breathe into you work that spark of originality that is so much in demand – your future will be assured in this writing field, and in others.

We will be studying:

- Knowing your newspaper's style.
- Choosing a suitable mood and style for each feature.
- Organising notes, preparing a rough outline.
- The opening. What you must put near the beginning.
- Language, paragraphs, sentences.
- Points the clients want to emphasise.

● Effective ways to close.
● Writing for cuts.
● Revising.

Knowing your newspaper's style

Most local newspapers are of the tabloid format, but not necessarily of similar content. Indeed, local newspapers are aimed at families, offering a lot of small news stories, and information that ranges from the achievements of local athletes, individual businessmen and women and their companies, to doctors' weekend rosters and what's on at local cinemas and theatres.

Judging whether your local newspaper is highbrow, middlebrow or lowbrow in its leanings involves reading through several articles. The tone will at once be obvious. But closer inspection is needed to provide the more precise information you need as a writer. Other professionals will be writing the headlines – editors, sub-editors – so you can concentrate on the text of each article. And you will notice that long words are rarely used, sentences are shortish, paragraphs the same. I have in front of me a short article that appeared in my own local newspaper, about a policeman who has an exciting life chasing sheep rustlers. The first three sentences contain, respectively, eighteen, twenty-four and twenty-nine words, and you will see that each is also a paragraph. The complete article consists of ten such sentence/paragraphs.

> An eagle-eyed policeman who has helped track down sheep rustlers has retired from the North Wales force.
>
> Det Sgt Ron Ewe of Everybach sacrificed many hours of his own time to catalogue more than 5,000 different sheep earmarks in his area.
>
> Now, Ron, 55, who won a Chief Constable's Commendation for his work, is set to start work as a market inspector with the RSPCA after 30 years public service.

A quick glance through the rest of the paper confirmed that most articles were in a similar style: sentences of about twenty-two words, each printed as a separate paragraph. However, one of my advertising features in the same issue consisted of sentences of a similar length, but paragraphs slightly longer – though rarely of more than two sentences.

The reason for these short paragraphs can be seen in the example. Most newspaper articles are printed in narrow columns, and a paragraph that would look perfectly manageable spread across the page of a book might take up a full newspaper column.

You will also find much 'journalese' in your newspaper. Officials 'quit in protest'. People 'look set to be celebrities' (as in the above example). Certain actions will have a 'devastating effect'. Floods will 'cause chaos' and put 'frozen food in jeopardy'. Councils will seek volunteers for 'jobs axe'. And people will 'clash angrily'.

All of those brief examples are typical of the short, snappy prose that allows an article to be produced using a minimum number of carefully chosen words that create a vivid picture in the mind of the reader. Take note of them, because some will be of great use to you. But also take care, for we are now entering the tricky waters in which you will fish for the right style for any given feature.

Choosing a suitable mood and style

When, in the next chapter, we look through our notes and write an advertising feature for good old Bert and Mabel Deli, we will use several bits of information to help us choose the right style.

Bert and Mabel will each have a certain outlook on life. It might be cheerful, noncomittal, sober or sombre. Their shop will probably – though not certainly – reflect that outlook. And then there will be unwritten convention – delicatessen articles are written in one way, hotels in another, and nightclubs in a style that would suit neither.

Examples will show exactly what I mean.

The first two show how totally contrasting styles can be used to write about two very different occasions in the world of music and entertainment.

This one was written for the North Wales Music Festival:

> Wales is rightfully thought of as the home of the Eist-
> eddfodau, but there are other musical occasions which are
> of great importance, and which provide rich programmes

for music lovers.

The North Wales Music Festival is a fine example. Performed in the cool, acoustically superb interior of St Asaph's beautiful Cathedral – with the occasional performance at a different venue – the Festival has been held annually for the past twenty-one years.

The following piece announced the opening of a modern discothèque. (The names have been changed, as they used to say in Dragnet, to protect the innocent.)

Acme Leisure have hit the North Wales seaside resort town of Everybach with a resounding bang, and a brief but memorable taste of fire and brimstone.

The impressive Beverly Hills nightclub is a phoenix rising from the dying embers of the doomed Cinders Club, and is reputed to be Wales' first, £1 million discothèque.

Different occasions, different venues, very different styles. (And completely different from Ron Ewe's 'newsy' story.)

The first is leisurely, with several long words creating a feeling of peace and elegance – and also giving the impression that the sentences are much longer than the second example (not so). Acme Leisure's nightclub piece, on the other hand, has more of that snappy, journalistic style. Although the newspaper will be read by all, this piece is aimed at the younger set, and so has been couched in language to suit.

Here is one more example that again shows a different style, but which is included because it will demonstrate other points that come later in this chapter. Once again, the names have been changed.

Bill and Olive Salt opened Blackbeard's Bistro in Upper Down Street, Everybach, in June, 1991 and for this lively husband-and-wife team it was much more than just another business venture.

The Vale of Clwyd is a very large step indeed from the Mediterranean or the Caribbean; yet Bill and Olive, former captain and cook respectively on a succession of luxury yachts sailing those exotic waters, are finding the change exciting, and rewarding.

Finally, when deciding on the mood of the piece you are writing (lively, leisurely, upmarket, racy), your overriding concern must be to inject it with optimism. Always accentuate the positive. Your clients are successful, they make the best garden gnomes, give the best facials and pull the most refreshing pints of real ale.

If you put it any other way, you are neglecting your duty.

Organising notes – preparing a rough outline

When I suggested writing your interview notes in paragraphs with ample space between them (Chapter 4), I did so because I do just the opposite – and pay for it!

Written in the ideal way, you have a chance of getting most of the information given to you in its correct place. On the other hand, I simply start at the top of a fresh page, find information coming at me from all angles and without any semblance of order, and finish up with arrows and asterisks and underlinings and notes scribbled up and down the edge of the page.

My first task when I sit down in my office is to read through my notes and bring order to that chaos. From those taken during the trip to Bert and Mabel's delicatessen, the result would be something like this:

- Coleslaw Delicatessen, 54 Upper Down Street, Everybach.
- Bert and Mabel Deli. Bert sole proprietor.
- Previously café on Lower Down Street – don't mention.
- In food business all life.
- Bought premises early August, opened mid-September.
- Alterations by William Fixit, Builders, Sparks, electrician.
- New kitchens, shop with two cold counters, interesting old signs.
- Aims: old-fashioned personal service and quality.
- Usual delicatessen fare, plus little-known quality brands, and home-cooked pies, sausage rolls, quiches.
- Cheese specialists.
- Staying small, retain control of quality.
- June Swift, local athlete, weekday help; daughter Deirdre Deli at weekends.

Once I have fathomed which bit of information goes where in the general order of things, I spend a few minutes considering how I will tackle the feature – because from those brief notes I will produce my 500 words. The general style will have been decided when in front of the client. But now I am about to create a story in that chosen style, and when you have reached this stage I suggest you write a brief outline. It need be no more than a series of scribbled notes.

You will need a beginning, middle and end. I usually add a short introduction and a brief conclusion.

I have already spoken several times about an advertising feature consisting of the past, the present and the future: what your clients have done, are doing, and intend to do. But although your story is in that sense chronolgical, your most likely approach will be to:

- Give brief but accurate details about the present.
- Go back to fill in the past.
- Come forward again to continue and complete the story of your clients' current activities.
- Conclude with your clients' future plans.

At the close you will often repeat one or two details that appeared in the beginning – clients' names, business name – but done in a way that makes the ending sound perfectly natural.

The opening – what you must put near the beginning

Kipling tells of the six honest serving-men who taught him all he knew. Their names were, 'WHAT and WHY and WHEN, and HOW and WHERE and WHO'. As an advertising feature writer you need to commit all of those to memory, and in particular the five Ws.

If you go back to the last of the samples on style you will see that:

- WHO = Bill and Olive Salt.
- WHAT = Blackbeard's Bistro.
- WHERE = Upper Down Street, Everybach.
- WHEN = June 1991.

56

All of them were revealed quite naturally in the first sentence.

The WHY will usually be explained when you delve into your clients' distant or immediate past, and the HOW – if you need to use it – brings your readers from the past into the present. For example, it might show how a builder created his business from scratch with the aid of hard work and the Enterprise Allowance.

Of the features I write, the Salt example is unusual in that it adheres strictly to journalistic principles: four of the five Ws are where they should be. The two previous feature examples – the North Wales Music Festival and the Beverly Hills – are more typical, as they open with descriptive introductions that contain few hard facts.

This is my style and it is instantly recognisable (within the local community). But even though I am allowed some latitude, I must still get those essential facts in early. So the next paragraph in the Beverly Hills feature continued:

> Opening on November 8, the Beverly Hills is situated in
> an ideal location on the corner of Hollywood Street.

Language, paragraphs, sentences

This is already familiar ground, as you will have taken into account all I said earlier and studied the way your newspaper's features are written. But within those vaguely delineated boundaries you will have room to create a style which is constantly interesting, and which succeeds in getting across to your readers the particular points your client is hoping you will emphasise.

Short sentences and short paragraphs are the unwritten rule. But never be afraid to use a reasonably long sentence or paragraph if you feel it is needed. And to avoid monotony, throw in the occasional very short paragraph. This can be just one word.

Emphasis

A word is emphasised if it comes at the beginning or end of a sentence.

That's easily demonstrated if I repeat what I've just said, in a different way:

A word at the beginning or end of a sentence is emphasised.

In the first version, the word that will linger in the reader's mind is SENTENCE. While in the second version, the emphasis has clearly shifted to EMPHASISED.

Be descriptive

It's easy to overdo adjectives and adverbs, yet without them a feature can fall flat. In that earlier example piece (CHOOSING A SUITABLE MOOD) I call Bill and Olive Salt a 'lively' husband-and-wife team. They sailed 'luxury yachts' in 'exotic' waters, and have found the change (to a shore-based business) 'exciting and rewarding'.

Even when talking about a waste disposal firm, you will find something to enliven your feature. One firm I know opened industrial units in a former piggery, and without being crude there was ample opportunity to inject some humour.

You can use a play on words – even puns if they are not too outrageous. I used a play on words when I wrote about a firm of solicitors. I said:

> Old firms, however venerable, are not necessarily good;
> while many of the better practices, which may have
> established their reputations by being in tune with modern
> thinking, are not necessarily old.

In a short advertising feature there is even room for brief quotations or anecdotes, and these will certainly colour your story. Good books to help you are *The Faber Book of Anecdotes*, Everyman's *Dictionary of Quotations and Proverbs*, and the *International Thesaurus of Quotations*, published by Penguin.

Always be specific

You will find yourself saying, for example, that 'among other things, Bill Fry has run a chip shop'. But 'things' is not a specific word, and it would be much better to say, 'among other business ventures'.

Always select exactly the right word

'Tasty' is in itself descriptive, but if we want to describe Mabel Deli's pies we might instead choose 'savoury', or 'well seasoned', while Bert's wines are probably 'fruity', 'mellow' or 'full-bodied'. *Roget's Thesaurus* in any of its many versions will help here, and the *Reverse Dictionary* from Reader's Digest is also excellent.

You will always have the problem of not repeating yourself, even in an article of 500 words, and you can come close to despair when you are writing your third feature in six months about the same business. No noticeable change; the company still produces garden gnomes. Just a fresh feature required – with the emphasis very definitely on fresh.

Objective

Finally, I'm going to close this section with perhaps the most important point of all (that's why it's at the end!). You must always be objective, rather than subjective. This must be obvious in the way you construct your feature, and you, the writer, must never intrude.

Here are some examples:

You must never say, '... as I entered the dining-room of the Plucky Duck... ' but instead say, '... as you enter... ' or, '... on entering... '.

You should never say, '... Bert Deli told me... ' or, '... Bert Deli said to me... ' but instead you must say, '...Bert Deli said...' or, '...said Bert Deli... ' or, '... as Bert Deli commented... '.

You should not say, '... I found the ante-room charming... ' but, '... visitors find the ante-room charming...'.

After a while, it all becomes second nature.

Points the client wants emphasising

You can repeat yourself *ad nauseam* and, although you'll certainly emphasise your point, you'll probably destroy all interest. So, simple repetition won't do the job – although you may mention particularly important points more than once.

Positioning helps, as was demonstrated by placing words at the end of a sentence. If you want to emphasise something, put it near the beginning of the feature and, for good measure, repeat right at the end. Another good idea is to associate the concept with something familiar that immediately creates a picture. For example, Bert and Mabel Deli have a shop, '... where any grandmother would feel at home...'.

Quotations from your client are very effective.

'... I believe there is no point in doing something unless it's done properly, and I intended to set up a Beauty Salon to the highest standard I could possibly achieve... '

So said one of my clients, and I emphasised the quality of her business by opening the feature with that quotation.

In another feature, a business had its excellent location emphasised by the creation of an opening paragraph that stated: 'It's not often that a residential home can be discovered in its own, three-quarters of an acre grounds, yet within easy reach of town, beaches, supermarkets and shops... '.

In summary, emphasis can be achieved by:

● Some repetition – not overdone.
● Positioning – at the beginning and/or the end of the feature.
● Association. Link the concept to be emphasised with a familiar and preferably much-loved stereotype.

Effective ways to close

The close of a feature must leave the reader with a feeling of satisfaction. If, at the same time, you can leave an indelible impression in the reader's mind – this is a business to be visited at the earliest opportunity – then you will have pleased your clients.

Finally, if you have achieved both of these aims and done so in a manner that satisfies you, the writer, then everyone is happy.

Well, perhaps. Or, not quite, because there is still one nasty little newspaper trick that can destroy that carefully thought-out conclusion, which we'll talk about in the next section.

In my short stories, I often link my conclusion to something that happened or was said near the beginning. Let's go back to Bill and Olive Salt. This was the opening of the feature:

> Bill and Olive Salt opened Blackbeard's Bistro in Upper Down Street, Everybach, in June 1991, and for this lively husband-and-wife team it was much more than just another business venture.
>
> The Vale of Clwyd is a very large step indeed from the Mediterranean or the Caribbean; yet Bill and Olive, former captain and cook respectively on a succession of luxury yachts sailing those exotic waters, are finding the change exciting, and rewarding.

And using the link idea I concluded by saying:

> All, it would seem, appreciate the fine fare and excellent wines provided by Bill and Olive Salt; a long way from the sea, now, but a dedicated and versatile couple deservedly riding the crest of a wave.

Another example along the same lines. The opening had a number in it that's usually associated with bad luck:

> For the past 12 years the Llanrhaeadr sports and Recreation Society has held a midsummer Miri Haf, or Gala Day.
> This year, the 13th, is no exception...

While the close was linked to it on a more positive and satisfying note:

> Either way, why not make a prior visit to the palm reader? Crossing her palm with silver might just reveal – in advance – that this years Miri Haf in Llanrhaeadr is going to be your lucky day!

Another excellent way of closing is to ask your client for an interesting quotation designed for that purpose:

> 'If you're eating out this Christmas,' John Plump said, 'then do think seriously about the Falstaff Inn. Our festive

> menus are delicious – and we'll even greet you at the door
> with a welcoming glass of champagne!'

You can use your closing paragraph as a summary; this was from
a car road test:

> All in all a car that compares more than favourably with
> close competitors such as the Hot Rod X and Hot Rod Y,
> and for the sheer joy of its handling and road-holding,
> beats them hands down.

A straight statement is another effective way of ending your
feature:'without doubt, the Roxy nightclub is the newest and live-
liest in town'.

Or you could use an anecdote: 'John Smith took the wrong turn-
ing on a Sunday afternoon drive, and was surprised to find himself
in the car park of The Black Cat. He's been a regular at this super
country inn ever since.'

Writing for cuts

Nothing annoys a writer more than seeing bits chopped out of his
work. Yet if you have written 500 words and the sub-editor finds
there is only room for 350, something must go. What usually happens is that the last paragraph is neatly excised. Snipped off.
Deleted. And so that wonderful, satisfying close, ends up in the
wastepaper basket.

The realisation that this can happen leads us to another feature-
writing fundamental: important facts are always put at the beginning. This is one of the reasons for the five Ws. Even if everything
except the first couple of paragraphs is consigned to the wastebin,
there'll still be enough left for readers to get the essence of the
feature. So, important facts up front. The WHO, WHAT, WHY,
WHERE and WHEN get progressively less important the more
you write. And although you may linger over your last paragraph,
create a satisfying close that links to the beginning by using an
excellent quotation and at the same time manages (for emphasis)
to repeat the name of the clients and their business, remember it
may all be for nothing.

Well, not quite, because you'll still get your cheque.

Revising

Some people have a revision plan, which is not at all a bad idea. If you know what you're looking for, you are more likely to find it than if you merely read through your feature to see if there's anything 'wrong'.

A revision plan might go something like this:

- In conjunction with your original notes taken at the interview, make certain that you have included everything in your feature.
- Referring to your finished feature, make sure you have got your clients' names, and the name of the business, exactly right – consistently, all the way through.
- In conjunction with your notes, check, then double check, all dates.
- Look for spelling mistakes and literals (typing errors).
- Look for repetition.
- Look for sentences where the meaning isn't clear, or even totally wrong.
- Look for mixed tenses.
- Look for subject and verb disagreeing.
- Look for hanging participles: '... having decided on a colour scheme, the dining room was completed in fourteen days... '.

(Who decided on the colour scheme?)

And when you are satisfied that you have checked your feature as diligently as you can against a list akin to this, take one final read through to see if there is anything you can improve. Because always, always, you must write at your very best.

7

WRITING – THE FEATURE

In this chapter I'm going to take you, step by step, through the writing of our advertising feature about Bert and Mabel's Cole-slaw Delicatessen. But before I do, you might like to re-read the interview in Chapter 5, and the summary of the interview notes that appears in Chapter 6, and using those as your guide have a go at writing the 500-word feature on your own.

When you've finished, use the revision plan at the end of Chapter 6 to check what you have written. Then, put your version to one side, read through this chapter, and see how your effort compares with mine.

Writing the feature

For most people, the worst part of any writing is the blank page or screen they are faced with at the outset. And if you're anything like me, you will probably make a couple of false starts before you get a piece with which you feel you can live. My false starts tend to be mostly in my mind. I stare at the screen, compose an opening paragraph in my head, reject it, try another, jot down just a word or two, then delete and do some more deep thinking. Usually, I'm aiming for something general. Pearls of wisdom, if you like, which in some way are related to the feature I am about to write.

Take Bert's delicatessen.

His aims are to give old-fashioned service, and quality goods. Now, you can't get much further from that aim than a modern clothing boutique with its racks of garments and deafening music.

So I toyed with that idea for a few minutes, and came up with:

> If life goes in cycles, then sometime soon we're going to
> see an end to shops where music makes thoughtful
> selection impossible, and the only way to get served is to
> serve yourself.

I believe there's some truth in that. Life does indeed go in cycles, and before too long the circle will be complete and we'll be back to shops where you actually get personal service. If I'm right, then it will because people like Bert Deli have made the move – or, conversely, have refused to budge – and that thought leads neatly into the continuation:

> In Everybach, the change is already noticeable, and if you
> make your way to number 54, Upper Down Street, you
> will find yourself in a modern delicatessen that manages
> to look old-fashioned in the nicest possible way.

Two paragraphs written, and how are we getting on with our five Ws?

Well, so far we've got the WHERE and the WHAT – though the latter not in great detail. But at least readers already know that we are going to tell them about a delicatessen, and they know where to find it.

And in the next paragraph:

> And Bert and Mabel Deli are more than proud to be running
> a delightful shop where any grandmother would feel at
> home.

... which not only takes care of the WHO, but gives me the opportunity to introduce those few descriptive words that – I feel – neatly sum up or epitomise what Bert and Mabel are trying to do.

In PREPARING A ROUGH OUTLINE in Chapter 6 you will remember I suggested the chronology should be juggled slightly, and that the second step in your story could be a flashback. We've reached that stage now, so I'll give the readers a bit of background information, and bring them gently back to the present with HOW and the WHY of the Coleslaw Delicatessen.

Bert Deli has been in the food business all his life, so when he founded the Coleslaw Delicatessen, he knew exactly what he was doing.

Mind you, common sense also played a big part. If you can't get the produce you want, then it stands to reason that other people can't either. And when Bert and Mabel had to hunt far and wide for cold meat for a summer salad, they realised there was an enormous gap in the market.

The premises were easy to locate.

A former ladies' fashion shop had come on the market, and after planning permission had been granted for a change of use, the Coleslaw Delicatessen was off the drawing-board and into the construction stage.

Main contractors were William Fixit, Builders and, ably assisted with the electrical work by Sparks, they completed the work in record time.

Bert and Mabel bought their premises in early August. By mid-September they were open for business, and within days they found themselves diversifying owing to popular demand.

You'll notice how I'm garnishing the hard facts so that they become more attractive and interesting. Bert did tell me that he had to drive, '... three miles to get top quality cold meats... ', and I've used that fact but painted a picture by talking about, '... hunting far and wide for cold meat for a summer salad... '.

Similarly, '... off the drawing board and into the construction stage... ' is dramatising facts, '... completed in record time... ' is a little plug for the contractor and electrician, and, '... within days they found themselves diversifying by popular demand... ' suggests instant success.

Right. The five Ws are taken care of, so now it's time to go into the delicatessen and tell the readers what it's like, what's on sale, and what's special about this new shop.

The shop itself is double-fronted, and the interior is well laid out and exceptionally bright. Two cold counters contain a wonderful selection of fresh delicatessen fare – cold meats, dishes of exotic salads, goat's milk in handy containers, natural yoghurts, and a wide range of cheeses – while elsewhere on shelves and convenient centre islands

there are cereals, pulses, herbal teas, essential oils for use
in aroma-therapy, and a selection of natural remedies.

But if you are looking for something that lifts the
Coleslaw Delicatessen right out of the ordinary and into
grandmother's good books, then you really must try
Mabel's delicious pies, sausage rolls and quiches.

Bert's aim from the beginning has been to provide
quality goods, and old-fashioned service. He and Mabel
provide the one without any effort, for it's in their nature,
while for the other – quality goods – Bert travels the
country to buy the very best from little-known sources.

Few of the names on the shelves will ring a bell, but if
you want savoury pickles and relishes that are free from
all preservatives, artificial colours or flavouring, then try
the Coleslaw Delicatessen.

The lunchtime sandwich bar was a diversification
opened by popular demand, and offers white or wholemeal
sand-wiches with dozens of tasty fillings.

In that section I used the information Bert gave me, and my own
observation. I tried to present it in a logical way, taking the reader
from the shop front to the interior, going from the general – the
layout, two cold counters – to the particular: some details of the
extensive range of fine foods.

Then I concentrated on what makes the Coleslaw Delicatessen
different: '... Mabel's delicious pies, sausage rolls and quiches...',
and Bert's efforts to provide not just a personal service, but goods
that customers are unlikely to get in other local shops.

I finished with a short paragraph about the diversification described earlier.

The staff must be mentioned:

If you call in during the week you will probably be served
by well-known local athlete, June Swift, while at weekends
Deirdre Deli will be helping her mum and dad.

Now, as I've already written 513 words, I must decide on the close.

I wonder how you handled it? I must confess I'm a bit of a
sucker for the 'link' close. In short stories, by the way, it's known
as the 'gimmick' ending: something that contributes to one of the
main conflicts is instrumental in arriving at the solution. But that's
inexcusable digression.

Here's what I chose.

> And even if you're not a grandmother you will be
> entranced by ancient signs, drawn to the tea that's stacked
> behind the counter in rich dark tins, and those well-stocked
> cold counters will convince you that in the Coleslaw
> Delicatessen you've discovered a gourmet's home from
> home.

Re-reading

I have done no revision on this piece other than a read through to
see if, as it stands, it would please Bert and Mabel. With your
critical eye, your notes, this feature and perhaps your own attempt
in front of you, you will no doubt pick holes in what I have done.
I hope you do.

You will certainly notice one or two omissions. For instance,
Bert told me he specialises in British and Continental cheeses,
and that customers can grind their coffee beans on the delicatessen's machine. I mentioned neither.

You will find as you get involved in this business that often
there is just not enough breathing space in the words allowed.
There are times when something must be left out, and then it's a
case of using your judgment. This raises another point. You are
writing a promotional feature, which is fine when you have something outstanding to promote. But what are you supposed to do
when you visit – for example – a dingy little pub with peeling
brown walls and malodorous cloakrooms?

The answer is that if you must lie, lie by omission; simply leave
out anything that is without a single redeeming feature. As for the
rest, write like an imaginative estate agent – or at least, as they
wrote before they were regulated. A pokey little room anywhere
becomes compact, cosy, or snug. Drab decor can be sensible, or
no-nonsense. A pub at the top of an impossibly steep hill occupies
a superb, elevated position with panoramic views. And a guest
house overlooking a busy main road is conveniently close to the
shops, or enjoys an enviable position close to all amenities.

8

HOW TO DEAL WITH REPEAT FEATURES

In many ways, writing a second or third feature about the same business can be more difficult than writing the original. There is an excitement about taking rough notes and using your eyes and ears, then converting what you have written and observed into a lively story full of original thoughts and imaginative phrases – for, make no mistake about it, good advertising features can be very good indeed.

Somehow, everything tends to fall flat the second (or third) time around. And writing a feature from another person's notes can be even more trying.

When making your own notes, you tend to part-write the feature in your mind as you scribble in your pad. The act of creation has begun, and you return to your office with the urge to start writing at once, while those half-formed ideas are still fresh.

By contrast, when a proprietor or manager hands you pre-written notes about a business, the words lie dead on the page. Later, you have not only the onerous task of correcting faulty grammar and organising disjointed information into some sort of order, but you must breathe life into what are essentially alien thoughts.

Nevertheless, despite all those minus points I rarely reject prepared notes. For one thing, they do save time at the interview by allowing you to discard questions for which you already have the answer. If any argument should arise over the accuracy of facts and figures, names or dates, you can produce those notes as an indisputable source of – presumably – reliable information.

In this chapter we will look at how to handle:

- Repeat features.
- Refreshing your memory (using original copy).
- The second interview.
- How to rehash.
- Rewriting your clients' copy.

Repeat features

Repeat features can come to you at any time, and will certainly come to you regularly if you succeed as an advertising feature writer.

As I mentioned in BUSINESS TO BUSINESS in Chapter 1, your newspaper will probably have regular slots in which businesses support each other over an eight- or twelve-week cycle. This means that, for this page alone, in a single year you could write four features for each of twelve businesses – in other words twelve features, each one rewritten four times!

Although your work does become easier – if less interesting – with each draft, you do need to take extra care with your facts. It's all too easy to leave dates unchanged, retired staff still working merrily away behind the counter, or (as I once did) a divorced couple still happily married.

Refreshing you memory (using original copy)

Once you get word that you are going back to do a second feature, your first job is to dig the old feature out of your files (or print a copy from disk) and refresh your memory. Even after three months or so you will find that Bert and Mabel immediately come alive again, literally springing off the printed page with their dedication to old-fashioned personal service and top-quality goods – and quite often you find yourself glowing with pride at the way you handled the feature.

You will also notice sections that are not quite up to your usual standard – a fact that only becomes clear now, as you read after that three-month interval – and it's these bits that will be the easiest to rewrite because you will be keen to improve.

In the case of the Coleslaw Delicatessen, when glancing through the copy you will remind yourself of the shop's layout, and the particular points Bert emphasised: specialising in cheeses, home-cooked sausage rolls, pies and quiches, daughter Deirdre helping out at weekends, coffee grinder for customers to use.

Look at the introduction, and the carefully thought-out close. Can they be improved? Did you get enough information upfront, or were you a bit tardy? If you can answer yes to either of those questions, then already your task is lighter. You are beginning to *want* to rewrite the feature, which puts the magic of enthusiasm firmly on your side.

Finally, it's always interesting and worthwhile comparing your copy with the version that was printed in the newspaper. If cuts were made, perhaps you can make use of those unpublished sections this time around? You might even be reminded – with a feeling of anger – that your marvellous final paragraph got the chop when the sub-editor ran out of space, and determine to throw it back this time.

The second interview

There are two ways of approaching the second interview, and I've regularly used both. In the first you'll make your appointment in the usual way but, when you arrive at the business – let's assume it's our favourite delicatessen again – you tell Bert that you've got all the background information you need, you know how he started the business and what he has to offer customers, so all you need from him now is any changes that have taken place. Or you make the appointment again but, when you shake Bert by the hand, you tell him that although you realise you've spoken to him before, for the sake of freshness you'd like to treat this interview as if it were the first. The reason I favour – and recommend – this way of going about a rewrite is that, human nature being what it is, the information you get is rarely a word for word repeat of what you got the first time. Not only will there be subtle variations in the way Bert tells the same story, but he will probably come up with several interesting bits and pieces he forgot to mention on your first visit.

71

You will be getting a fresh slant on a familiar tale – and that's exactly what you need to enable you to write your second version.

Note the changes

Whichever way you choose to go about your second interview – in and out as quickly as possible, or the lengthier but potentially more productive way I recommend – you will be looking for changes. The most obvious is change of ownership, and a surprising number of repeat features are booked for this reason.

There are many others, and some of these can spring directly from plans mentioned in the first feature: the pub that was hoping to construct a children's play area in the springtime; the hotel intending to add extra bedrooms in the near future. Because you studied your copy before leaving home, and again when you parked your car, asking how such plans are progressing is a good way of breaking the ice. The client is flattered that you have remembered, and becomes talkative, and co-operative.

Bert and Mabel Deli had no plans other than to stay small enough to enable them to continue with their successful policies. But part-time help comes and goes, and it would be worth enquiring about June Swift, and Deirdre Deli. Are they still there? Are they married now, or away at university, etc?

No doubt Bert will have uncovered some more delectable pickles and jams produced in a remote country kitchen; the sandwich bar may have been expanded to include the provision of hot, takeaway snacks, and – again because of demand – a new section might have been opened, offering a range of body-building supplements for local enthusiasts, and natural embrocations and liniments for exercise injuries.

Style and emphasis

This is where direct feedback from the client is important.

Bert Deli received your copy of the first feature the day after you wrote it. All he was allowed to do before it went to press was telephone to correct any obvious mistakes. But the general tone of the feature might have been entirely wrong.

I've had clients tell me that all they wanted was a simple record of what they were trying to do; no fancy language, no flowery prose, just tell it 'as it is...' – and this is after I've sweated over a literary work of art that turned out to be entirely wasted on them. I've also had clients ask me to do everything I possibly can to refine, polish and enhance what they have given me; to 'create a real, proper story, you know how to do it, you're the expert...' – and still be dissatisfied when I've followed their instructions to the letter.

On this second interview you must ask your clients what sort of impression they thought the original feature created. Did they feel that it accurately portrayed their business (bear in mind that the way they see their business might not match your own impressions) and helped get customers in through the door?

If they were in any way dissatisfied, if they thought it was patronising, demeaning, insulting, too low-key, way over-the-top – then you must put things right for the second feature, and ensure that your clients continue to make use of your newspaper. Satisfied clients keep you in a job.

Although I've been accentuating the negative in the last few paragraphs, let me reassure you now: most clients are average people who have great difficulty writing a letter once or twice a year, which means that ninety-nine times out of a hundred they are delighted with what you write for them.

How to rehash

When you're in a rush, when it's Tuesday morning and you have ten – yes, ten – features to finish by noon on Wednesday, rehashing usually means altering the introduction, tacking on a different close and leaving the rest as it is. Here, I'm thinking particularly of general or Christmas features. When you describe what it's like to go shopping in a town that hasn't changed in the four years you've been writing for the *Weekly Smudge*, you have great difficulty being original.

Ah, you might think, but who's going to notice anyway? Well, possibly nobody except the features editor. But professional pride is at stake here, and knowing you have skimped the task is likely to leave you with a nasty feeling of guilt. So you will be relieved to hear that doing a thorough job is not too difficult.

Rewrite

Changing the beginning and ending means that you must rewrite completely up to four paragraphs. For the rest, it's rather like moving the furniture to give your sitting-room a new image. Take this paragraph from our delicatessen feature:

> Bert Deli has been in the food business all his life, so when he founded the Coleslaw Delicatessen, he knew exactly what he was doing.

The same information can be given like this:

> With many years experience in the food business behind him, Bert Deli was confident that he was doing the right thing when he established the Coleslaw Delicatessen.

Here's another example. This was the original paragraph:

> If you can't get the produce you want, then it stands to reason that other people can't either. And when Bert and Mabel had to hunt far and wide for cold meat for a summer salad, they realised there was an enormous gap in the market.

And this is the rewritten version:

> Knowing what people want, and making sure they can get it, is the secret behind every successful business; and from their own experience Bert and Mabel knew that their delicatessen would be a valuable source of fresh, wholesome foods.

If you turn back to the original feature and look at the old paragraphs in context, you will see that the replacements slot in neatly.

Rearrange

Now, it's not necessary to rewrite every paragraph. But if you change completely the beginning and the end of your story, select two or three further paragraphs for quite drastic trimming and shaping and do some light cosmetic work on the rest – you will find, on reading through the new version, that you've done a most acceptable rewrite.

By light cosmetic work I mean change some words or phrases – instead of a ladies' fashion shop being 'on the market' it could be 'up for sale'. Or use the same words, but alter the order – instead of 'main contractors were William Fixit, Builders', say that 'William Fixit, Builders, were the main contractors'.

It's as simple as that.

Rewriting your clients' copy

On all but the rarest of occasions, you will find faulty grammar and incorrect spelling in the copy clients provide. But before you do anything about that I suggest you work on their copy in one of two ways.

As notes

In the first I simply treat the clients' copy as an extra set of notes – which, of course, is exactly what it is. To bring everything together into one manageable chunk, I slot the extra bits of information I obtained from my clients at the interview – my own notes – into the correct places in the copy they provided, then move all the separate bits and pieces around until they are in the order I need for writing a readable story.

You will remember that the guide we used to arrive at this order was:

● Give brief but accurate details about the present.
● Go back to fill in the past.

- Come forward again to continue and complete the story of your clients' current activities.
- Conclude with your clients' future plans.

Then it's simply a matter of writing the feature from the bulky set of notes I've created – but making sure I use as many quotes as I can (clients are particularly proud of something they, or perhaps their managing director, have said), and any of the supplied paragraphs which are good enough to include verbatim.

As a raw feature

The alternative approach – one I always adopt when the copy supplied is particularly good – is to consider the clients' written material as the complete but raw feature, which now needs expert editing.

Again using my check list, I type their work into the computer, leaving it unchanged, but reorganised. Then I consult my own notes, write several paragraphs using that information (which – because I asked the right questions – is always different and additional to their supplied copy), and insert these into the correct place. After that it's just a matter of completing the feature by revising according to the plan given at the end of Chapter 6, which takes care of faulty grammar, incorrect spelling, and almost anything else that could possibly be wrong.

9

WORK ORGANISATION 1

This book has been written with the intention of showing writers how they can make money by writing advertising features for their local papers. People in widely diverse situations will read it.

At the one extreme there will be the young, single people who, with application, should be able to earn enough money to keep themselves in reasonable comfort. At the other end of the line there will be people who are married. Some of these, too, will be able to earn a full-time income from writing advertising features that will, on its own, be enough to enable them to support their families.

There will be a host of readers who lie between these extremes. Single parents of both sexes. Short-story, article and novel writers who need an additional income to make ends meet. People who earn their main income from a source other than writing, but are hoping to make useful additional money. And others who are in no need at all, but enjoy their hobby and would appreciate the pocket money advertising feature writing can provide.

The one thing all these people now have in common is that as they embark on this career – part- or full-time – they are leaving behind the cosy world that allows them to take time over their writing, and are entering one where deadlines loom. So, to a greater or lesser degree, their time must be organised.

In this, and the following chapter, I will be discussing the way your work must be organised if you have embarked on advertising feature writing – either on its own or with other forms of writing – as a full-time career. But the same principles will apply if you are struggling to fit your writing hobby into the grind of a busy working life.

In this chapter we will look at:

- Organisation.
- Meeting deadlines.
- Manuscript presentation.
- Delivery of work.
- Copies to clients.
- Coping with the emergency feature.
- Storing completed features.
- Organising time as workload increases.

Organisation

Let's assume that advertising feature writing is your sole, full-time occupation. At the beginning of this book I quoted a typical workload of five features a week. To complete those I said I need – when things go according to plan – one day for interviewing, and another for writing. But there are times when that workload can double, and when it reaches that stage, good organisation is of the utmost importance.

As an advertising feature writer for a weekly paper, your deadline will probably be midweek. Let's say it's Wednesday. On that day, all the features to which that deadline applies will have been posted, faxed, or delivered by hand, and you will either see or talk to your features editor.

In your office, on your Monthly Work Sheet (see Appendix), you will have some features that are now current, say two or three. So, in theory, you know the volume of work you must complete by the next deadline – Wednesday, one week from today.

Your features editor is continually getting feature briefs from staff in the advertising department (who are not too worried about your difficulties in meeting deadlines), and you might still be getting additional work – due in Wednesday – as late as Monday of the same week. This leaves you with the task of organising last-minute interviews with people who never understand the urgency, while ensuring that you still have sufficient time to write features that are not just well crafted, but sparkle with originality.

78

Meeting deadlines

Usually, you will be given a feature with no instructions other than the deadline and it will be left to you to arrange the interview. Occasionally, there will be certain factors that govern when you can see your clients.

For example, in summer, features will often be booked when clients are about to fly off to the Bahamas, and you must see them early. Or clients are refurbishing their hotel, and you cannot see them until the work is finished. Or you need to see the clients in plenty of time, because your copy will be vetted by their head office.

In general, however, everything will be straightforward, and then you have two options:

A   You book all your interviews for Monday or Tuesday, and get up early on Wednesday to do the writing.

B   You organise your interviews for Wednesday afternoon and Thursday, complete the writing on Friday, and sit back knowing that if extra features are phoned through, you've got plenty of breathing space.

I have always used the first method and now strongly advise against it because it doesn't make good sense. Yes, I know that the computer can blow up, the power lines can blow down, I can get 'flu, food poisoning, lose my notes, oversleep yet still I stick to this appallingly risky routine.

Why do I do it?

Well, as far as I can ascertain, most freelance writers are remarkably similar. They know their capabilities and so, faced with this kind of work, instead of counting forwards from the day they get the feature brief in order to establish how soon they can finish, they count backwards from the deadline to work out how late they can start.

This seems perfectly logical. After all, those calamities I've just mentioned happen to other people, never to us. Nevertheless, although I've got away with it up to now, my advice is to adopt method B, and get features completed as they come in. That way, you have always got time in hand – unless an emergency feature lands on your desk, of which more a little later.

Manuscript presentation

Most people reading this book will be familiar with the way work should be prepared for submission to magazines, newspapers and other publications, and advertising features should be treated in exactly the same way. That is, the copies going to the *Weekly Smudge* should:

- Be typed or printed on good quality A4 paper, using a sharp black ribbon.
- Be typed or printed in elite or pica type. If you use a computer with a dot matrix printer, always use letter quality (LQ), or near letter quality (NLQ), never draft.
- Be double spaced.
- Be clearly headed with your own name, and the name of the feature.
- Have each page clearly numbered.
- Have MF (more follows) at the foot of every page except the last.
- Have END and the number of words at the foot of the last page.

Little explanation is needed for the first three points, but your newspaper may issue their own guidelines about the fourth – the heading.

I do it this way:

THE COLESLAW DELICATESSEN   (31/12/93)   Sheriff/1

Contact: Bert Deli 0123 456789

The date is there for my convenience, the contact details are put in at the request of the newspaper. You will find both of great help when you amass a large number of completed features going back over several years. If you use a typewriter you would put this heading on your first page, leave it off all others, and type the required information (MF, END, number of words) at the foot of the relevant pages.

Using a computer, you would probably set up a template with headers and footers, leaving blanks for the business name, date, and contact details.

Delivery of work

The way you go about this will depend on how far your home or office is from the newspaper, and what the newspaper wants.

First-class post is usually reliable, but a disadvantage is that your deadline is brought forward: you must have your copy ready for the post the day before it's needed at the newspaper.

Using your own fax machine is as quick and as cheap as a phone call, but if you need to go to an outside machine – many local businesses provide this service – it can cost £1.50 or more for a single A4 sheet. And, double spaced, a 500-word feature runs to at least two sheets. I find a fax machine wonderful for short messages, but very often the print quality at the receiving end is poor. So for a 500-word feature that might include important facts and figures, my feeling is that fax is not good enough. In the past I have had to waste time clarifying points over the phone; except in an emergency, I never use them.

Delivery by hand is ideal. You know your copy is arriving at the right place at the right time, and you get a chance to talk to your features editor. Very often you want to explain why you have included certain points in your feature, and discuss with the editor those sections you feel your client is likely to comment on, or query. In addition, the editor will be able to discuss with you the new features being handed out, and tell you about special requirements.

There are other reasons why delivery by hand can help you as a writer. In the beginning, to all the newspaper's staff you are just a voice on the telephone. This is perfectly all right. You can run your business without ever meeting a member of the advertising staff, or the features editor, and never have any problems. But my own feeling is that if work begins to dry up, and a dwindling list of features must be shared between two or three outside writers, it's the familiar face that is going to come off best.

It's probably a little unfair (to editors, who would argue the point anyway) to say that it's not what you know, but who you know. So let's just say it's often a case of being in the right place at the right time. If you are sitting down talking about features with the editor, it takes but a second for one or more feature briefs to change hands – and saves the newspaper a lengthy phone call.

Delivering your copy by hand also gives you some insight into the workings of a busy weekly newspaper. You may get no further than the reception area, but even there you will see the comings and goings of staff, watch clients calling in to discuss layouts, and catch glimpses of the vast open-plan offices filled with desks and computers that epitomise the modern newspaper's work area.

Am I talking about inspiration? Perhaps I am, but I also feel it's a process of familiarisation – for more than one freelance feature writer has gone on to become a staff reporter, or even a features editor.

Copies to clients

Few clients are happy if a feature you have written appears in the newspaper before they have seen it. And letting a client look at the feature before it goes to press means that, no matter what eventually appears in the paper, they will know you have done a first-class job completely in accordance with their wishes, and instructions.

For example, in Chapter 6 I mentioned that editors who run out of space often cut from the end. Without your copy, clients will assume that the printed ending is the ending you wrote, whereas with a copy in front of them they will at once realise that your original version has been shortened.

But the main reason for giving clients a copy of the feature is to ensure all the facts are correct. Where dates are concerned this is of vital importance, and so, at the bottom of the sample FEATURE WORK SHEET, you will see 'CLIENT APPROVED: yes/no' – and I always make sure it's the 'no' I can delete.

An alternative to the written copy is to read the feature over the phone to your clients, and when I started writing features that's what was recommended to me. But it can be a lengthy process, and a lot of people simply cannot concentrate sufficiently to make sense of telephone dictation. Also, there are no safeguards. There is rarely a record of a telephone conversation, and when errors slip through it's difficult to say if the client or writer is to blame. It can also be expensive if your costs are not reimbursed.

Nowadays, I always take clients' copies with me when I deliver the originals to the newspaper. They are in envelopes bearing the clients' address, and I hand them in for posting, thus ensuring that the newspaper knows a copy has been sent.

The copies going to your clients will be exactly the same as your original – carbon copies, in fact, if you use a typewriter. If you use a computer, it's quite all right to send a draft copy (printed on a good ribbon), and when you are doing a lot of work with a deadline not too far away, this can save valuable time.

Coping with the emergency feature

An emergency feature can differ from a normal feature in one or more ways:

- The deadline is always immediate: the feature must be done ASAP.
- There is often no alternative but to do a telephone interview.
- It's not always possible to get a copy to the client before typesetting, so the onus is on you to be absolutely certain of your facts.
- You will almost certainly have to fax or hand-deliver the feature to the newspaper.

As we've already seen, a normal feature can become an emergency for a number of reasons. Usually it's because the client has been unable to see you, but because of circumstances – the date of the official opening of a retirement home, for example – the feature cannot be delayed.

There will be occasions when you are ill and have to cancel an appointment. Every so often, there will be confusion: your features editor thought you had been told about the Coleslaw Delicatessen, when in fact you never received the brief.

A true emergency feature – in my opinion – is one that the features editor has got from the advertising department or the editor at the last minute, and has passed to you with instructions to proceed with all haste.

The four points raised at the beginning of this section cover most of what you need to know. The deadline is obviously upon you, but if you possibly can, do a face-to-face interview. Because the client is not getting a copy, make absolutely certain that you are accurate in your note-taking. In both types of interview – face-to-face and telephone – read dates, times and spellings back to your client to ensure they are correct.

When you revise the feature, take especial care over checking it against your notes. If you are faxing the feature to your newspaper, make sure you have a good ribbon in your typewriter or printer – that way you have done all you can to ensure the faxed version is readable. Even better, deliver the feature by hand – you can usually claim expenses for your special trip.

Storing completed features

Carbon copies

The simplest way of storing your features is to print off three copies: one original, one for the client and one for your files. Cheap manila folders will serve to hold your copies, and one method is to keep each month's output together so that at the end of a year you have twelve labelled folders.

If you wish, you can use a cross-reference system: you will note that there is space for a number and date at the top of the sample Feature Work Sheet, and this number can be entered on the front page of the completed feature. The date refers to when you received the feature brief from your editor – the actual date you wrote the feature will be in your feature heading, as described above.

Newspaper clippings

The alternative to this system is to cut each feature out of the *Weekly Smudge* as it appears. Because newspaper print is so small the features take up much less space than your original, and by judicious clipping you can usually stick two average features on each side of an A4 sheet. Storing will be exactly the same, but your monthly manila folders will be much slimmer.

Computer disk

In many ways, the computer disk is the ideal storage medium. On a 3.5in. floppy disc formatted to 720k there is enough room for about 140 features – that will give you some idea of the space this method saves. Most computers will do a screen dump – an exact, printed reproduction of the screen – so if you clear the screen, list or catalogue all the files on a full disk and do a screen dump, you will have an accurate printed record.

I label all such records with the disk number – NEWS/001, etc – and keep then in plastic covers in a ring binder. If I need to find a back feature, all I need do is flip through the file. You can use a Feature Work Sheet cross-reference system in exactly the same way as you did with printed copies: simply enter the date from your Feature Work Sheet at the beginning of the relevant feature stored on disk.

All of these methods have worked for me in the past, and all enabled me to locate any feature within seconds, and if necessary link it to the information on the original Feature Work Sheet.

You may come up with your own scheme – one possibility is to use a simple card index containing details of feature and work sheet (with the alphabetical dividers reversed, and relabelled with month names); another is to use a computer database which will allow a lot more information to be stored, and permit rapid resorting.

But be warned: if you decide on this latter course, you will probably need to be licensed under the Data Protection Act.

Organising time as workload increases

If you reach the stage of working for two or more newspapers, you will find yourself with a lot of work, and many miles to be travelled. Usually you will find that two papers will cover adjacent areas, with perhaps a small overlap. Occasionally you will write the same feature for both papers – either in the same week or month, or at different times.

Efficiently organising this increased workload is mostly a matter of adhering rigidly to your chosen system.

If your workload has increased but you still work for just the one newspaper, then that's all there is to it. However, if you have been taken on by another newspaper, then you will need to pay particular attention when filling in the first part of your Feature Work Sheet – Newspaper and Contact – and ensure that you keep the two newspapers' work sheets in separate files (or separate sections of the same file). You will also need your wits about you when meeting clients: it's all too easy to announce yourself as being from the *Weekly Smudge*, when the feature you are working on is actually for the *Weekly Blot*!

10

WORK ORGANISATION 2

Throughout the book I've been talking about Feature Work Sheets and Monthly Work Sheets (I call that one a Pending Sheet, by the way – it usually lasts about five or six weeks) and how you must claim for expenses and so on, and this is the chapter where – I hope – all this begins to make sense.

There's also a brief discussion on the way this business of writing local advertising features can be used to make a great deal more money in the national marketplace. Here's what you will find:

- Claiming expenses.
- A typical monthly claim.
- Income tax.
- National insurance.
- Feature Work Sheet.
- Pending Sheet.
- Conclusion – where to go from here?

Claiming expenses

I've put this before Income Tax and National Insurance because you're not liable for those unless you've got an income of some kind. And it's your monthly claim that will – in part – determine the size of that income.

To recap on what I said in Chapter 1, the *Weekly Smudge* is likely to pay you a lineage rate based on 100 printed lines and a pro-rata payment when you exceed that. They will also reimburse petrol and telephone expenses. How you are expected to claim will be dictated by the idiosyncrasies of your particular newspaper. Some firms demand detailed claims listing dates, newspaper, page number etc on pre-printed forms, while others just ask you what you wrote and the number of words.

A typical claim might look like this:

John Novice,
Upper Down Street,
Everybach.

31 December 1993

Features Written December:

1	Coleslaw Delicatessen, 500 words:	£18.00
2	Old Banger Garage, 400 words:	£16.00
3	Wrinkly Lodge, 500 words:	£18.00
4	Lazy Leisure, 350 words:	£14.00
	Telephone calls, at cost:	£ 3.50
	Car, 110 miles at 25p/mile:	£27.50
	TOTAL	£97.00

The more detailed version will take longer to complete, but the essential information required will be the same: lineage, mileage, telephone costs, because it's on those that your payment is based.

A glance at the figure being reimbursed for mileage allowance in the above sample shows that, particularly if you live in a remote area, simply driving from A to B yields a considerable profit. So if you claim for, say, 50 miles travelled when you actually interviewed your client on the telephone, you are going to be £12.50 better off before you've written a word.

It's a temptation. After all, expenses are there to be fiddled – aren't they? The answer to that is, no, don't do it.

You are being taken on trust to provide your newspaper with an accurate record of the actual miles you travelled on newspaper business. And while they will, with some grumbling, pay you twice for a journey if you had to go back because the client was out the first time, if they catch you claiming for a journey you didn't make your job is unlikely to last very long.

Income tax

The detailed examination of a professional writer's liability for income tax is beyond the scope of this book, and if your income warrants it I would suggest you employ the services of a good accountant. However, what I can do is give you some idea of the expenses that may be deducted to arrive at your taxable income.

Personal allowances change almost with the moon's phases: there is the individual personal allowance, and the married couple's allowance which brings in something like an additional 50%. But those apply equally to employed people, and it's through the other allowances that the self-employed writer gains an advantage.

The list is massive, and includes: secretarial services; telephone and postage; all stationery requirements; office equipment, including batteries and maintenance; reference books, magazines (when necessary for the running of your business); lighting, heating, rent and rates (according to the number of rooms used solely for business purposes); professional services (accountant); car running expenses, including insurance, road fund tax... and so on, and so on.

The important words to remember are, 'wholly and exclusively laid out for the purposes of the profession', because if an expense falls within those guidelines, then it can be deducted from your income to arrive at the final, reduced figure – your Taxable Income.

Keep all receipts, and an accurate record of all your outgoings on a day-to-day basis. If you do employ accountants, you will hand all your financial records to them at year end.

There is now a simplified tax return system and, if adopted, a self-employed writer need submit to the inspector of taxes only a brief statement detailing income and expenditure. However, accurate records must still be kept, as they must be available for inspection. One disadvantage of the simplified system is that any tax due becomes payable at once (in two stages), whereas when full accounts are submitted there are complicated procedures which allow payment of tax to be deferred – again, outside the scope of this book.

There is much more, and you will find excellent guidance of particular relevance to writers in *The Writer's Handbook* (Macmillan /PEN), and the *Writers' and Artists' Year Book* (A & C Black).

National insurance

As a freelance (self-employed) writer you will need to pay Class 2 (self-employed) national insurance contributions. They can be paid by monthly direct debit through your bank, or by quarterly billing. In addition, there is a Class 4 contribution rate for which you will become liable if your annual profits reach a certain level. But the important point to note is that the sums specified refer to profits, not income – and your liability under Class 4 is 50% tax deductible.

Feature work sheet

A sample of this sheet, and the Pending Sheet, will be found at the end of the Appendix. Both were designed to suit my needs, and have been altered slightly over the past couple of years. If you use them as a guide to design your own, the essentials to include are the newspaper, feature, contact and text (length of) details. I use the number at the top right for cross-reference purposes, and the date I enter there is the date the features editor passes the work to me.

I've already mentioned the Client Approved details right at the bottom. Sometimes, for one reason or another, clients fail to receive a copy of the feature. If you make a habit of deleting either Yes or No, you can always check to see if you actually sent one. The notes section is self-explanatory. I use it for everything, from the special reasons for a particular feature to directions on how to get there.

Pending sheet

I've shown this one with two newspapers on the one sheet. That's because most months I would get a lot of work from the one, and a lot less from the other – there was usually plenty of room. If you strike lucky and get two or more papers feeding you features as fast as you can write, then it might be a better idea to use separate sheets.

Again, you can adapt to suit your needs. I place a tick in the APP/T column as I make firm appointments, but I'm getting the feeling that it's unnecessary. Any day now I'm likely to amend the sheet.

Conclusion – where to go from here

At the very beginning of this book I said that, 'I want you to sit at home writing, and I want you to get paid for what you write'. All freelance writers know how difficult that can be. Close study of magazines and newspapers will show you that even 'big name' journalists and broadcasters are not too proud to peddle their literary wares in the open marketplace – and, yes, they do get the occasional rejection.

This is the kind of competition new writers are up against but, although it makes the struggle that much harder, it also makes success oh, so sweet. Because if your humble article or story is accepted by a major national glossy magazine, you know that your work has been chosen as the outstanding piece from perhaps a couple of hundred hopeful submissions – many from well-established writers.

I'm going on at some length about this business of national publication because that is the pot of gold at the end of the rainbow for most aspiring writers. I'd like to believe that this book, for many, will be the means to that end. Through the door it has opened you will find yourself regularly writing a wide variety of features to tight deadlines. This will improve your vocabulary, increase fluency, and very quickly establish your individual style.

The first door leads to others, and you should always approach every advertising feature with a view to submitting a different

91

version of the story to a national magazine.

Here are two examples.

For one advertising feature, I was sent to a country bakery run by a young woman. It specialised in cakes baked the old-fashioned way. The advertising feature was 500 words long, and earned perhaps £20. I expanded the article, and sold it to The British Baker – with two black and white photographs – for £140.

I did another advertising feature on the opening of a night-club. It earned £20 from the newspaper, and a revised version of the same length – with colour transparencies – sold to *Club Mirror* for £195.

It always helps to have photographs available, but if you cannot take your own you will often find that businesses have a stock of prints or transparencies you can use. Often, anyway, it's best to submit the text first when approaching a magazine, and let the editor know that there are photographs available, if required.

Although the rules pertaining to an advertising feature still apply – the five Ws, a structure with important information at the beginning, brief flashback and then the body of your story – your style of writing will need to be adjusted. Often this entails little more than lengthening paragraphs to suit the wider format of a magazine page. Lively quotations always add interest, and you will certainly have the space available to use more imaginative writing. Remember that people always enjoy reading about people – how they got where they are, what they are doing, their hopes and ambitions.

Advertising feature writing, then, is an invaluable source of article ideas, and perhaps that's one answer to the question, 'Where do you go from here?' But your own plans may be even more ambitious and, if you are working on a biography or a blockbuster, then I think it's better if I leave you with one final thought.

Because of this book, it's unlikely that you now match Samuel Johnson's definition of a blockhead. In order to go on to achieve that greater success without which you will never feel truly satisfied, you must leave Sinclair Lewis, surely, the last word.

APPENDIX

Advertising features promoting similar businesses tend to follow a pattern. Although the following samples are written in my style, the contents will give you a good idea of what you will need to include when you come to write about a garage, a pub and so on. This appendix contains the following samples:

- Sample features.
- A shop.
- A garage.
- A health club.
- A Feature Work Sheet
- A Pending Sheet
- A newspaper feature example

Sample features

A shop

"If you want it, we've got it" is the kind of slogan that invites customers to come in and put the claim to the test.

If they do, it's served its purpose – and if the goods the customer is seeking happen to be anything to do with cycles, or DIY, they're almost certain to walk out having made a purchase.

The business behind that confident slogan is Bill's Bikes and DIY, which has been trading in Upper Down Street, Everybach for the past 5 years.

Over the years this successful family business has set

its sights on providing quality goods backed by a friendly service which serves two separate sections of the Everybach community.

Bill Benn, born in the Lake District, is a qualified plumber and, after completing his National Service, he settled in Yorkshire where he met his wife, Jenny. In 1986 he had set his sights on taking over an established hardware store in Everybach. When that failed to materialise, he opened his business selling and repairing cycles.

The next two years were spent getting established and by 1988 it was obvious that larger premises were needed. The move to Everybach came in that year, when Bill's Bikes opened at the premises it occupies to this day.

Initially the business was solely occupied selling cycles and accessories, with a fast and efficient repair service run from a workshop on the premises.

In 1990 the family decided to diversify the operation, and introduced a new section in the Everybach shop offering a wide range of DIY requisites.

Cycles of all kinds are still a speciality and, as well as a budget range by Unicrank, Bill's Bikes stock top quality mountain bikes, sleek racing machines, even the less frequently seen tandems and tricycles.

Bill Benn, himself a keen cyclist, joins son Willy in maintaining the quick and efficient cycle repair service – everything from a puncture repair to major rebuilding or an insurance quotation – which has been operating since the early days.

On the DIY side the firm sticks rigidly to its slogan. Most of the goods required by the DIY enthusiast are stocked, including sand and cement, electrical products, nuts, bolts and ladders. If you want it, then Bill's Bikes and DIY have got it!

As a safeguard, the family involvement includes the in-shop guidance offered by Jenny Benn, who stressed that, if Bill's Bikes don't stock the goods required, she usually knows another store that does.

Just to make purchases easier, Bill's Bikes and DIY offer a year-round Christmas Club facility that also comes in handy for birthdays and other occasions.

A garage

Over the years the family car has gradually evolved from the simplicity of the Austin Seven into a highly complicated piece of technology that needs specialised care and attention.

Keeping pace with technology, recent legislation makes special care no longer a matter of choice, but a legal requirement.

For the past five years or so Steve Grease has been keenly aware of the changes affecting the car industry. At Everybach and at the fine modern premises at Truck Lane, Otherbach, his Stretchit Cars has continually set the standards by which others are judged.

No longer is it necessary to seek out the franchise which deals with your particular make of car. At Truck Lane, Stretchit Cars' Multi Make Service Centre is equipped and staffed to service and repair all makes and all models, from the simplest of saloons to the latest off-road 4 x 4s.

With that skilled attention come a number of additional services that show why Stretchit continues to be a highly successful business.

For example, washing and steam cleaning is automatically included whenever a car comes in for servicing or repair.

Computerised documentation means that servicing dates are carefully recorded, and Stretchit Cars takes on the responsibility of advising customers when their next service is due.

Three clean, modern servicing bays are available at Stretchit and these are controlled by Service Manager, Wal Kin. Wal has two skilled mechanics working with him, and between the three of them there is something like 50 years experience in the trade.

Computerisation has found its way into the workshops, too, and the latest hi-tech equipment – the Nosweat Analyzer – has simplified fault diagnosis and fine tuning down. This not only eliminates most mistakes, but also cuts down customer costs by providing a speedier service.

Inevitably, the first-class repair and servicing facilities

offered by Steve Grease have resulted in a great deal of repeat business, and Stretchit Cars – an established company that takes a pride in offering a truly professional service without gimmicks or worthless surface gloss – also handles servicing contracts for many well-known local businesses.

In addition, there are exhausts, tyres and batteries at prices that compare favourably with those offered by specialised outlets – and like everything else at Stretchit Cars, they are fully guaranteed.

A health club

Tucked snugly away on Upper Down Street, Everybach, the Gin Sling Health Suite and Beauty Salon is a delightful establishment offering a range of services that will appeal to the modern woman who takes pride in her physical appearance.

Located at 1, Muscular Buildings, Gin Sling is owned by Lorna Doom, who is currently studying Beauty Therapy at Duff College.

There is an extensive use of pine and brick throughout the two-storey premises, the reception area is bright and comfortable, and receptionist Carmen Inne is always available to book appointments and help with enquiries.

A doorway with beaded curtain leads to the two, ground-floor solariums, which are equipped with sunbeds featuring Bronze-it Tubes and facial panels and offer fast, safe tanning.

The first-floor Sauna is a 4-seater and, alongside, there is a spacious beauty salon which is the heart of Gin Sling. Here, professional beautician, Clare Skin, is available to give manicures, pedicures, a variety of waxings – full leg, ankle to knee, bikini line – and Gin Sling has a range of revolutionary facials which tone and revitalise. Depilation is also available, eyebrows can be shaped and trimmed to perfection, and there is an excellent make-up service using top-quality products.

Prior to using the Solarium or taking any of the services on offer in the Beauty Salon, skin tests are available. The elevated Spa Bath is in its own, private room, and offers an invigorating bathe for up to three people.

Excellent shower facilities are available; towels, robes and hairdryers are provided, and there is also a vanitory unit on the first-floor landing.

In October this year Lorna opened a Slimming Club, and those women who joined – 50 at the last count – have each lost up to a stone in weight.

In addition to the provision of health and beauty services, Lorna sells a full range of beauty accessories. There is also an attractive range of jewellery for sale, and refreshments are available throughout this pleasant health suite and beauty salon.

FEATURE WORK SHEET   No *2/94*   **Date** *13 Jan*

NEWSPAPER: *Weekly Drudge*   **DEADLINE:** *19 Jan*

CONTACTS: *Fiona Blue-Pencil*   **PHONE:**
Everybach 800

FEATURE: *Coleslaw Deli*

ADDRESS: *54 Upper Down St*   **PHONE:**
Everybach   *0123456789*

CONTACTS/INTERVIEWS: **DATES:**   *17 Jan*
Bert/Mabel Deli

PHONE:
0123 456789

TEXT: *500*   **COMPLETED:**
18 Jan

NOTES

Recently taken over.

Best times – mid morning, late afternoon

CLIENT APPROVED: Yes/~~No~~

DESPATCHED:
18 Jan

FEATURES PENDING

THE WEEKLY SMUDGE

BUSINESS NAME	APP/T	LOCATION	WORDS	DEADLINE
Camera Kit	✓	Otherbach	800	5 Jan
				12 Jan
Coleslaw Deli	✓	Everybach	500	19 Jan
Stretchit Cars	✓	Everybach	475	✓
Bills Bikes	✓	Everybach	750	26 Jan

THE WEEKLY BLOT

				5 JAN
				12 JAN
				19 JAN
				26 JAN

99

HOW TO WRITE ADVERTISING FEATURES

A newspaper feature example

Christmas *in Prestatyn*

How much is that doggie? — a giant toy that's guaranteed to delight a small child this Christmas

Mayor will switch on seasonal cheer

By John Sheriff

In Prestatyn Christmas is officially due to start when the Mayor switches on the lights on Tuesday December 8.

This year, in addition to the 30 foot Christmas tree in the High Street, there will be some 250 smaller trees on retail establishments throughout the town.

For a lot of people, though, Christmas in Prestatyn means much more than bright lights, Christmas trees and that sparkling festive spirit. It means excellent shopping, a compact shopping area that's never too crowded, good parking facilities – sadly, no longer free - and personal service that takes away at least part of the strain.

Convenience

Shopping in Prestatyn inevitably focuses on the High Street, though it must be remembered that there are side roads with clusters of shops which add to the charm and convenience of shopping in this resort town.

The beauty of Prestatyn is that it's the town that has everything.

Presents for tiny tots are available from a number of shops dealing in babywear. One such is The Rocking Horse, which also stocks prams, and many others have selections of toys both cuddly and cute, along with others that educate as well as amuse.

For the older child Prestatyn is a wonderland. If there is a musical interest there are shops selling the latest in CDs, records and cassettes.

Stereo cassette players are the present most teenagers would put near the top of their list, and J Gibbons has them in all shapes and sizes, plus TVs for the living room, the bedroom, even for the beach.

While if a child of any age is hoping for a bicycle for Christmas, then pop along to W and S Cycles who can supply the bike, plus the other bits and pieces that can transform the modern youngster (and parent!) into a replica of the Tour de France rider.

Fashion shops abound in Prestatyn. Dress For Less has an excellent range of ladies and children's clothing. Ladies Pride stocks high quality fashions for the modern woman.

INDEX

INDEX

Paragraphs, length of, 52 –53, 57
Paxman, Jeremy, 33
Payment, methods of, 7 – 8
Pending sheet, sample, 99
Pens, 30
Pens versus word-processor,
17 – 19
Plan, revision, 63
Play on words, 58
Presentation of manuscript, 80
Printed information, from clients,
32
Punctuality, 34

Questions,
Applying for the job, 23 – 24
When interviewing, 37
*Quotations and Proverbs,
Dictionary of,* 58
*Quotations, International
Thesaurus of,* 58
Quotations, 58

Rearrange, how to, 74 – 75
Recorder, tape, 30, 40 – 41
Refreshing the memory, 70 – 71
Rehash, how to, 73 – 76
Repeat features, 69 – 76
Reverse Dictionary, 59
Revising, 62 – 63
Revision plan, 63
Rewrite, how to, 74 – 76
Roget's Thesaurus, 59
Routine, working, 15 – 17

Screen dump, 85
Second interview, 71 – 73
Sentences, length of, 52 – 53, 57
Small business interview, typical,
43 – 49
Specific, how to be, 58
Staff, involved in advertising
features, 10
Structure, feature, 56

Style,
choosing, 53 – 55
repeat features, 72 – 73
the newspapers', 52 – 53
Support advertisements, 3

Tape recorder, 30, 40 – 41
Telephone,
costs, 7, 88
interview, 41 – 42
Thesaurus, Roget's 59
Thomas Fuller, 31
Track record, 13 – 14
Typical,
commission, 26 – 27
small business interview, 43 – 49

Words,
choosing the right ones, 59
play on, 58
Working routine, 15 – 17
Work delivery,
by fax, 81
by hand, 81 – 82
by post, 81
Work Organisation 1, 77 – 86
Work Organisation 2, 87 – 92
Work Sheet, sample, 98
Work time, 16 – 17
Writer's Handbook, The, 90
*Writers' and Artists' Yearbook,
The,* 90
Writing,
for cuts, 62
planning and preparation, 51 – 63
skills, 4 – 7
the Feature, 64 – 68
time, example, 16
time, optimum, 17
Ws, the five, 56, 65, 66

103